Donn A Whitacre

ARCHITECTURAL DELINEATION

"I see through my eyes—not with them."
William Blake

ARCHITECTURAL DELINEATION
a photographic approach to presentation

Ernest Burden

McGraw-Hill Book Company

New York   St. Louis   San Francisco   Düsseldorf
Johannesburg   Kuala Lumpur   London   Mexico
Montreal   New Delhi   Panama   Rio de Janeiro
Singapore   Sydney   Toronto

Contents

Preface

Are today's methods of delineation as up to date as the buildings they depict? Perhaps not, considering that a Renaissance artist would feel quite at home in today's studio or classroom. It was the Renaissance artist who witnessed the birth and development of the concept of perspective, a concept which had eluded mankind for centuries. This development of perspective happened simultaneously with the discovery and application of certain principles of optics which led to the earliest form of camera, the camera obscura.

Here for the first time one could trace a true-to-life image on the glass of the camera back. By the year 1685, the camera was completely ready and waiting for photography, however, its use and development was not realized for 200 years, until the development of sensitized paper. The camera obscura, though, remained the useful and popular tool of the artist for many years. Eventually, this simple device was replaced by an elaborate system of mathematical and geometrical constructions. This method, developed during the Renaissance, persists to this very day. Fortunately, through the development of its counterpart, the camera has taken greater strides in helping mankind to see and record the world he lives in.

To delineate means to draw, trace, or outline a form, but taken in its broadest sense it means to depict accurately. It is this concept which must be restored to the field of presentation. The time consuming, archaic methods of plotting perspectives have no place in our modern world. The alternative of approximated "eyeball" perspectives is not satisfactory to depict today's concepts of building design. What is truly needed is a quick, accurate, and flexible system and here the camera provides a ready answer. The ideas and examples provided in this book will contribute towards restoring delineation to its proper perspective. This can best be described as a drawing which is a precursor of a photograph of the completed project.

Most architectural renderings precede the actual building by several years. Some projects may never become realities for one reason or another. Others may undergo such extensive revisions that the design, as originally conceived and rendered, may not resemble the finished product.

It is with this in mind that I thank each architect listed in the design credits section following the text for permission to publish the renderings of his project. I extend this thanks equally to those architects who provided drawings of their projects done by other delineators. And I must express my gratitude to those delineators for their fine contribution to this book.

I appreciate the assistance given to me by those directly concerned with the production of this book, including those who helped make and re-make the photographs.

To my friend and editor Bill Salo I want to express my thanks for making the entire production of this book a very rewarding and valuable experience.

To my wife Karen I owe much, for her encouragement and understanding, and for typing the manuscript no matter how many times a revision was needed.

Ernest Burden

PART ONE
Basic concepts

Chapter 1

The camera and perspective

The Renaissance was an age of rediscovery. Artists tried to depict material things within a framework acceptable to the human eye. During this period an artist-architect, Leon Battista Alberti, tried to express the relationship of a structure in real space to one depicted on his drawing board. He stated that his depictions would be like holding up a window to the world, and on this window he would be able to trace pictorially the true dimensions, the true colorations, the true shadings, the true existence of whatever scene he chose to hold his window up to. Alberti was talking about scientific perspective, yet he described what we know today as photography.

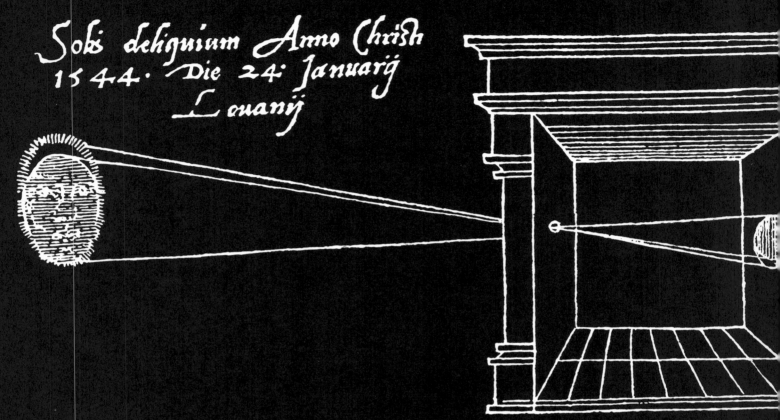

Solis deliquium Anno Christi
1544. Die 24: Januarij
Louanij

"When the images of illuminated objects pass through a small round hole into a very dark room, if you receive them on a piece of white paper placed vertically in the room at some distance from the aperture, you will see on the paper all these objects in their natural shapes and colors. They will be reduced in size and upside down, owing to the intersection of the rays at the aperture."

—The notebooks of
Leonardo da Vinci.

Camera Obscura

The invention of the camera obscura has been erroneously attributed to Alberti, Roger Bacon, and Leonardo da Vinci. It was, in fact, described by the Arabian scholar Alhazen before 1038, although knowledge of it can be traced back to Aristotle. The first published illustration of the camera obscura by a Dutch physician in 1544 described a method of observing solar eclipses. It was soon discovered that by this means one could see things going on in the street as well.

The camera obscura, in its original form, was the darkened room in a house. This is where the name originated, "camera obscura" meaning literally a dark room. The first significant improvement to it was the inclusion of a biconvex lens in the aperture to form a brighter image. The next improvement transformed the box-type camera into a reflex-type camera. A plane mirror at a 45-degree angle to the lens reflected the image the right way up onto a piece of oiled paper stretched across the opening in the top of the camera.

In 1685 the camera was ready for photography as we know it today. What was needed was a method by which the images produced by the camera obscura could be fixed. Louis J. M. Daguerre had for many years been trying to fix the images automatically instead of tracing them by hand. He used the camera obscura to achieve realistic detail and perfect perspective. He finally succeeded in developing a method of fixing the image on a polished silver plate. Details of the method known as daguerreotype were much publicized. No knowledge of drawing or manual dexterity was necessary. Anyone could succeed with the same certainty and perform as well as the author of the invention. This day, the nineteenth of August, 1839, stands as the official birthdate of photography. Many exclaimed in excitement, "From today painting is dead!"

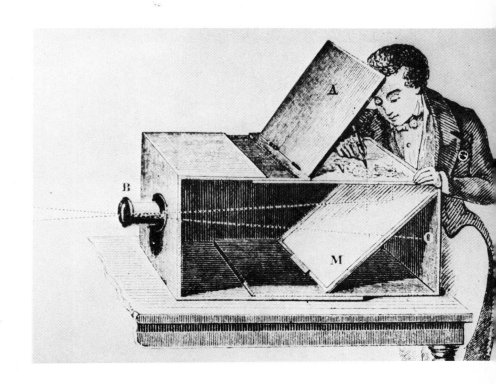

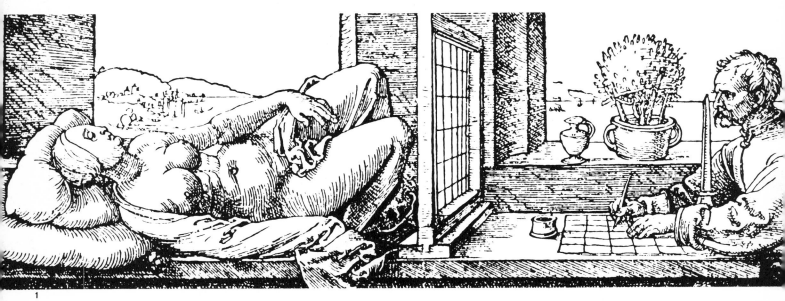

1

A Comparison of Systems

Vision is a process whereby light rays, reflected from objects outside, are received by the eye's lens. This lens condenses the rays to a point, from which the rays reemerge to focus a small, inverted image on the retina, a wall of light-sensitive cells. The retina transmits the light messages across the optic nerve to the brain, which comprehends these messages as a picture of the object. The brain automatically turns the image right side up and laterally correct.

Perspective drawing, or visual ray projection, is accomplished by drawing rays from the object to a point, called the station point. The rays are arrested on a plane prior to reaching the station point. This picture plane, however, can represent only one dimension of the object, and the plan view is the one usually chosen. The remaining information is obtained by additional projections and measuring devices.

Photography is the process whereby light rays from outside objects are received by the lens of the camera, which condenses them to a point. From the lens the rays of light reemerge and focus an inverted diminished image on the surface of a piece of light-sensitized film. Once exposed to light, this film is chemically developed to the point where the image on it can be comprehended as a picture of the object.

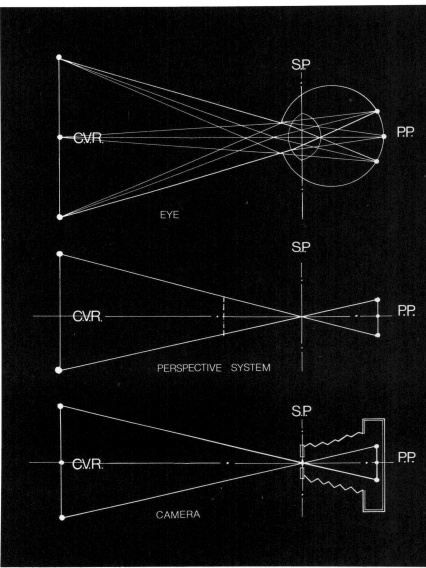

Any system of representation should reproduce, as nearly as possible, the eye's impression of the external world—a true representation of a three-dimensional object upon a two-dimensional surface. Neither the camera nor a mechanical system can ever do more than represent one instant of what the constantly moving eye can see. Alberti's window to the world was thus limited inasmuch as the artist could use only one eye and could not move his head. The drawing by Dürer (1) shows a device resembling an obelisk, used by artists to ensure a fixed point from which to draw. Starting from this station point, we can easily draw comparisons of the two methods of representation with that of human vision.

Station Point (SP)

That point from which the object is drawn. In human vision it is the lens of the eye. In perspective drawing it is the location of the observer, represented by a point in plan. In photography it is the location of the lens of the camera or, more specifically, the point within the lens system where the rays converge.

Picture Plane (PP)

In vision it is our picture of the object as formed on the retina. In perspective drawing it is an artificial device used to arrest the visual rays of the object before they reach the station point. It is represented in plan view by a line. In photography it is the piece of light-sensitive film within the camera.

Cone of Vision (CV)

The light-receptive cells of the retina of the eye extend in angles of 30 to 50 degrees vertically and about 100 degrees horizontally. Yet the eye gets a clear picture only within a cone of about 45 degrees. In perspective drawing it is therefore advisable to limit the cone of vision to 45 degrees, approximating what the eye sees clearly. In photography, although there is a wide choice of lenses, the kind called "normal" has a cone of vision of 45 degrees.

Central Visual Ray (CVR)

The central visual ray, or axis of the cone of vision, can be represented in any mechanical system by a straight line bisecting the angle. The central visual ray must be perpendicular to the picture plane for correct vision or representation of an object. In normal vision the system of sight is intact. In perspective drawing it is not. Here it is necessary to locate a picture plane, cone of vision, station point, and central visual ray in order to set up the perspective. It must be purposefully drawn in its correct relationship or a distorted picture will result. Although the camera is generally a fixed system, constructed so that the central visual ray will be perpendicular to the picture plane, there are many variations. Some cameras are constructed to allow changing these fixed relationships, thereby altering or controlling perspective.

Camera Types

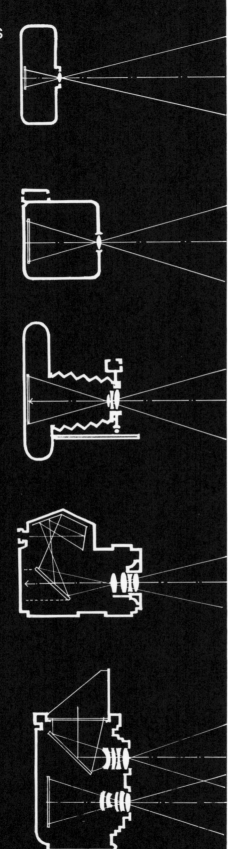

Subminiature Cameras

These are usually precision built and contain many features of larger cameras, such as a miniature reflex system for viewing. They are especially good for model photography work, as their small size allows them to be placed where others would not fit. The basic drawback is the small negative size, which limits enlargements in black and white. For color slides this is not a problem. Most standard films are available for subminiatures.

Fixed-lens Box Cameras

These are the most common of inexpensive cameras. The lens is ground to produce a sharp picture of anything from as close as 3 feet to infinitely far away. They are designed for the average type of snapshot and can be used for site surveys or any general picture. There is usually a separate viewing system, making critical work inaccurate. Some models do include automatic features such as exposure control.

Polaroid

These form a class all by themselves. Their unique feature is the built-in developing equipment which makes it possible to view a finished print just seconds after the shutter is snapped. These cameras are now so completely automatic that they have no adjustments at all except a simple light control. The user merely aims the camera, presses the shutter release, and proceeds to develop the picture. For general work they are quite adequate, providing a negative is not desired for future enlargements.

35mm Single-lens Reflex

With these popular cameras the user views through the lens itself, seeing the same image in the ground glass viewer that the lens transmits to the film. Focusing on a ground glass ensures accuracy for all types of work. These take only 35mm film and yield a large number of exposures per roll, making them economical for use with color. Again, the small negative limits the size of enlargements of black and white film, but for color slides this is not a problem. When a color-slide presentation is prepared, this camera is very useful for everything from site photos to critical copy work. Many accessories are available, including a variety of lenses.

Twin-lens Reflex

These widely used cameras have two separate lenses: one is coupled to a viewfinder and one takes the picture. This provides an image at all times in the ground glass and is very necessary for catching action. For other uses it is not an advantage, as there is always a chance of error (called parallax) between the two lenses. These take a larger-size film than the 35mm models and therefore are superior for black and white work. They are easy to operate and yield good results for most work. Accessories are available, such as wide-angle and Telephoto attachments.

Single-lens Reflex (2¼ Size)

These are based on the principle of the camera obscura, incorporating a mirror at a 45-degree angle to the lens, which reflects the image onto a ground glass in the top of the camera. This allows through-the-lens viewing up to the moment the picture is taken. They offer the same large film size as the twin-lens reflex, producing twelve 2¼x2¼ pictures on 120 roll film. Most models feature interchangeable lenses of all descriptions. The large, handy ground glass makes it particularly useful for certain techniques in coordinating architectural models with their sites.

View Cameras

The largest and most complex of all cameras are the view or studio cameras. They are usually limited to studio use due to their size. They can take large-size film in sheets depending on the size of the camera (4x5, 8x10, 11x14). A ground glass is mounted in a plane where the film will be inserted in holders when a picture is desired. This gives maximum quality of focusing and composing, although the image is upside down and laterally reversed. The bellows system is completely flexible, allowing the lens board, or the film plane, to be turned in any direction, thus enabling the photographer to create perspective distortion or to correct it to any degree he chooses.

Characteristics of Lenses

Most of the advanced camera types described above will accept a variety of lenses which change their angle of view. The lenses that most closely approximate human vision are constructed to receive and focus on the film a cone of light rays with an angular conical spread of about 45 degrees. These are called normal lenses. However, the term relates only to a specific camera type. For example, the normal lens for the 35mm single-lens reflex is a 50mm lens having an angle of view of 46 degrees. The normal lens for a 2¼x2¼ format reflex is a 70 to 85mm lens having an angle of view of approximately 45 degrees, and a 4x5 view camera uses a 150mm lens having the same relative angle of view.

Most wide-angle lenses cover a field of 60 to 75 degrees, although some go up to a full 90 degrees without apparent visual distortion. This type of lens lends itself to certain situations where space is limited, such as indoors or on narrow streets. It is used to capture wide panoramas or architectural models at close range. Certainly the architectural photographer must rely on it heavily.

The Telephoto lens is especially designed to photograph distant objects. The angle of view of most Telephoto lenses is from 10 to 20 degrees. It is useful when photographing a far-off site or people. However, for most applications the normal lens is sufficient and should certainly be the first lens to buy with any camera. Other lenses can be added as they are required.

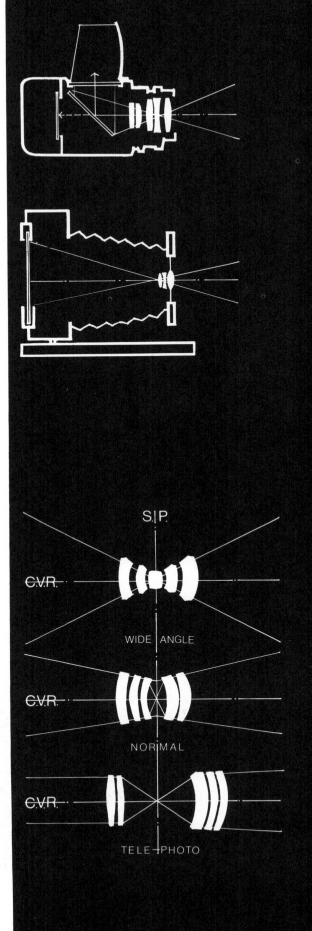

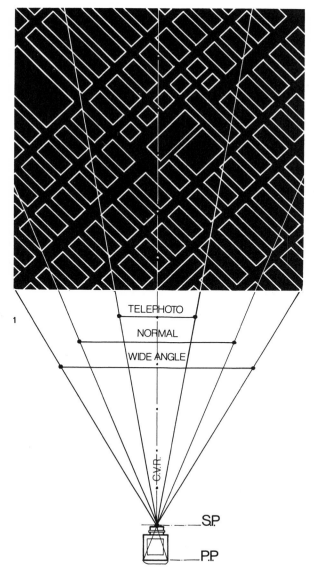

TELEPHOTO

NORMAL

WIDE ANGLE

C.V.R.

S.P.

P.P.

1

2

Fixed Station Point

At this point in the discussion let's put two theories to the test: one, that perspective is a function of station point, and two, that different lenses at a fixed station point do not alter the perspective appearance of a recorded view.

The diagram (1) is an actual block map of the heart of New York City. The station point for the camera was located on a rooftop several blocks away. With the camera set up on a tripod, three pictures were taken: the first through a 150mm Telephoto lens with an angle of view of 20 degrees (2); the second through a normal 85mm lens with an angle of view of 45 degrees (3); and the third with a 50mm wide-angle lens and a 60-degree angle of view (4). The three pictures were printed without enlargement, to indicate the full negative image. Then a section corresponding to the Telephoto frame was selected from each of the other two and enlarged to the Telephoto frame. The outline on these pictures indicates the area that was enlarged. It further illustrates the extent of enlargement of that area due to the angle of vision of each lens. The resultant three photographs (5,6,7) are identical. As long as the station point remains fixed, the three lenses will produce identical perspective images.

The second experiment was made by using one lens and changing the station point relative to the object. Three views were taken (8), each successively closer, and all three were enlarged until the object appeared the same size (9,10,11).

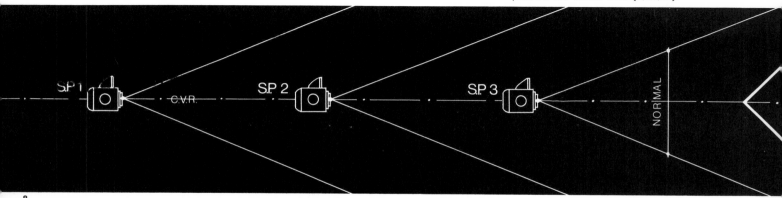

S.P. 1

C.V.R.

S.P. 2

S.P. 3

NORMAL

8

3

4

5

6

7

The view from station point 1 is flat with very little convergence and is similar in appearance to what we might expect from a Telephoto lens. The flatness is due entirely to the distant station point. The view from station point 2 is normal with a reasonable degree of convergence and looks like most images of structures we see every day all around us. The view from station point 3 is somewhat distorted in appearance, similar to what we are told to expect from a wide-angle lens. The extreme convergence is due only to the close station point. In short, perspective is the direct result of a single element: station point.

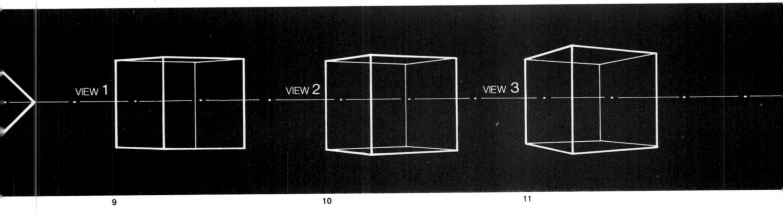

9   10   11

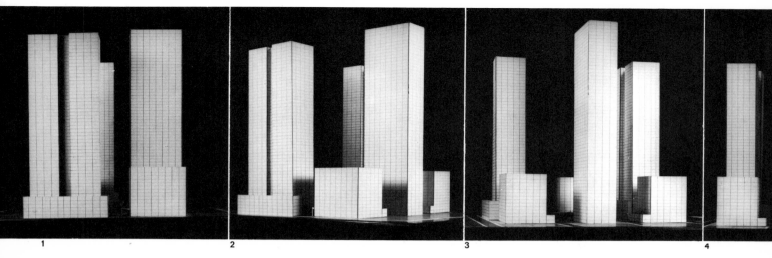

1 2 3 4

Changing Station Point

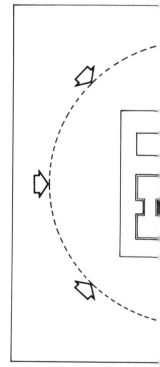

Architecture is fixed, immobile, and unchanging in form. To an observer, however, the appearance of a structure does change, because the observer is capable of motion. Therefore, the observer is the one who must be considered in any attempt to show a structure from different vantage points.

The changing relationships experienced by a person walking around a structure can be duplicated very easily. An architectural model was used to represent a group of buildings in a city block, and a camera to record the views of the observer. The model used was a box model of simple cardboard construction. On the surface was drawn a grid representing a curtain-wall window system.

Two photoflood lamps were used to illuminate the surface and a black backdrop was put behind the model for contrast. The camera was set on a tripod and elevated to a height that would approximate the eye level of a person walking around the building. In order to ensure a constant station point, the camera was fixed in position and the scale model was pivoted about its center point. This produced the same effect as if the camera had been on a circular track and circumscribed a complete arc around the structure. The results can be seen in the series of pictures above. Commencing from a flat, head-on view (1), the model was rotated,

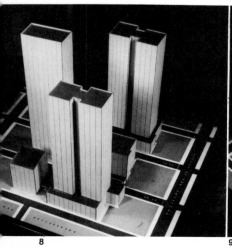

8 9 10 11

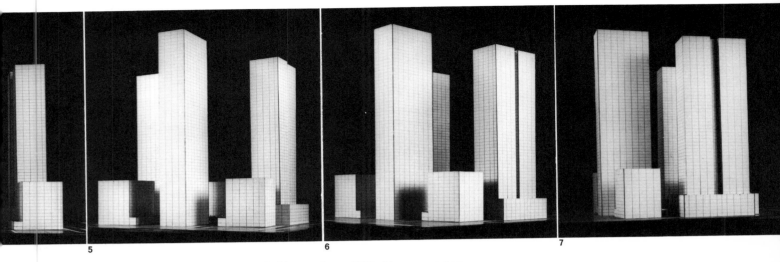

5   6   7

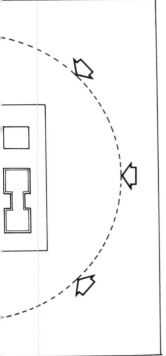

producing several oblique views (2,3). At one-quarter of the way around the model, another flat, head-on view (4) was recorded. Moving further around provided two more oblique views (5,6). Finally, at one-half the distance around, a view was recorded that was directly opposite to the first (7).

Studying the interrelationships made possible by the use of the camera should be an exciting change to the delineator. Previously he would have laboriously set up a perspective, only to find that a few more feet to the right or left of his chosen station point would have produced a more desirable result. To the architect wishing to study his project this exercise is invaluable.

The same demonstration was done for a high viewpoint. The camera was placed on an elevated tripod at a fixed distance from the model. In the same manner as before, the model was rotated through 180 degrees and a series of photos was taken (8–14). From this high station point the camera was tilted away from perpendicular, producing a third vanishing point. The result of this exploration will show you what to expect from the camera. You might even begin to consider exciting angles of perspective you would have hesitated to try before now. Do not feel restricted to a ground-level viewpoint. The three-point results you capture on film are as easy to work with as the conventional perspective.

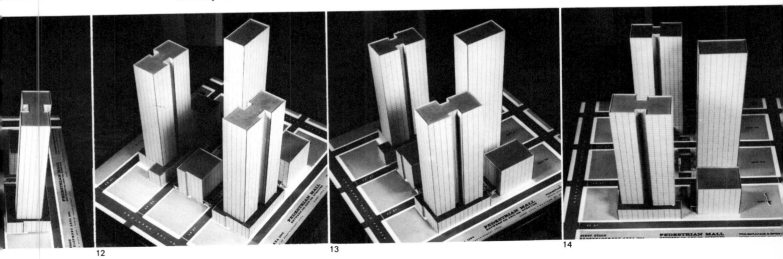

12   13   14

1

Eye Level

In the previous example the station point was kept constant and the camera positioned before the model was rotated. Remember, station point as a symbol occurs only in a plan view, whereas eye level occurs only in elevation. The two are inseparable. Station point represents your distance from the structure as measured orthographically in plan view, and eye level means your height above the station point, which can be measured only in elevation.

From a selected station point you might want to study the effect of a changing eye level. With a camera and a model of a proposed project this is a relatively easy matter.

The camera was placed on a tripod which had an elevator head capable of moving up or down with a crank. It also had the elevator shaft calibrated into equal increments to facilitate measuring the eye level. The results are shown here in four consecutive views (1), each an equal distance from the previous one in height. The camera itself had to be kept parallel to the vertical plane to avoid introducing a third vanishing point (2).

As mentioned earlier, the human eye is a closed system. All things look "natural" to the eye because that is our standard of judgment for "seeing." When we look up, things diminish upward, and when we look down, things converge downward (3). Yet this never bothers us because we are always within our frame of reference. However, when a photograph duplicates this process (of perspective convergence), we find it noticeably disturbing because it is outside our frame of reference. Therefore, a picture of what our own eyes see can be disturbing unless we view it from the correct distance and at the proper angle. This means from the same relative position that the camera was when it took the picture. Then the picture will appear normal again to us because it is much like the way we would see it ourselves.

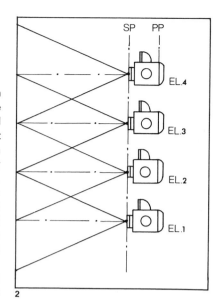

2

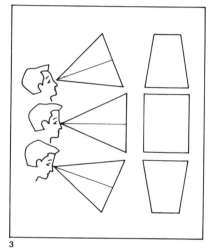

5

3

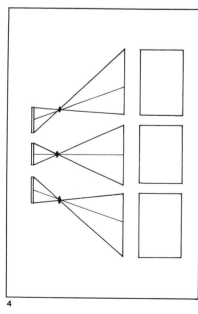

4

7

6

Any time the camera (4), and hence the film plane in the camera, is tilted out of a plane parallel to the object, a distorted looking picture will result. The vertical lines will appear to converge to a third vanishing point. This is a natural manifestation of perspective. The upper edge of the building, being farther away from the lens, will be accordingly smaller. There are ways, however, to avoid this. If the camera is held horizontally, distortion will not result, but the picture will not show enough height and will include too much foreground. The camera in the same position but with the lens raised will give a perfect photograph of the whole structure.

The camera most commonly used to control this situation is the view camera, having a lens which can be raised or lowered and tipped or swung. However, the two views shown here (5,6) (7,8) were taken with a 35mm camera with a special perspective control lens which can be raised or lowered. Normally such features are available only on larger cameras.

8

1

2

3

4

Camera Movement

People view most action in real life in terms of four basic sequences: the distant view (1), medium view (2), close-up (3), and extreme close-up (4).

A rendering is limited to one view from one location at a time. However, with the camera you can explore many possibilities within minutes. Viewpoint is no longer restricted to what is convenient or mechanically easy to construct.

When exploring a model, site, or building for possible viewpoints, consider these basic elements of the simple sequence: the distant view, the medium view, and the close-up. To these can be added the extreme distant view and the extreme close-up. In a sequential form these basics produce pictorial continuity, which may have little significance for the single rendering, but becomes the criteria for slide and film presentations.

The view which establishes the scene is the distant view. This can sometimes be very far away, locating an object in its surroundings. The medium view would be a "normal" view, usually encompassing the entire object or building within a well-balanced framework or composition. While the distant view is quite elastic, the medium view has little range and becomes sharply limited to the full-view or full-figure shot. It is also known as a transition view between the distant and close view.

The close view is more revealing of detail. It necessarily has focused on only a portion of the entire project, emphasizing entourage. This close view can also be stretched to an extreme close-up, or environmental view, where great attention to detail is necessary. The object has lost its frame of location and becomes immediate environment. In the sequence shown, movement was kept in a relatively straight line, as one would walk toward a building, up the street, crossing the street, and terminating with the main focus at the entrance. This is the basic formula of the simple sequence.

5

7

16

Perspective Systems

There are three systems of architectural perspective drawing. One is known as one-point perspective (5), where the object is parallel to the picture plane and those sides of the object that are at right angles to the picture plane recede to one vanishing point, while everything else remains parallel.

6

Another is known as two-point perspective (6). This system assumes a vertical picture plane upon which all vertical lines of the object appear vertical and parallel while all horizontal lines converge to vanishing points on a horizon at the same height as the eye level. Three-point perspective (7) assumes a picture plane inclined from vertical. Systems of horizontal lines still converge to vanishing points on the horizon, but now only the vertical line which is intersected by the camera axis remains vertical, while all other vertical lines converge to a vanishing point along this line. There are three vanishing points for systems of lines parallel to the three-coordinal axis.

1

Camera Movement and Composition

Seek a picture in the subject rather than of the subject. Search for composition first of all. The building will take care of itself if a sequence has been followed. Try to avoid the strict straight-line approach as if you were zeroing in with a zoom lens from the same spot. With each succeeding view, change direction, camera angle, or both. Again follow the basic sequence of a distant view showing the building in relation to its surroundings (1), a medium view framed within neighboring buildings (2), and a close view showing a detailed relationship to the immediate surroundings, including the street (3). Framing the drawing with a known landmark or with an existing structure helps establish scale of the new project (4).

2

3

4

Camera Angle and Framing

There are essentially three primary angles from which to choose: the straight-on normal angle, the high angle, and the low angle.

The low angle (1) necessarily places more importance on the foreground and creates drama. It is effective for showing a relationship between near and distant objects.

The high angle (2) usually reveals more than the usual eye level. It tends to emphasize pattern and compositional lines. Town squares and unique architectural groupings are usually best shown from the high angle.

Framing the low angle is generally an easy matter. The high angle can only be composed properly since no framing element exists. However, the straight angle has a multitude of possibilities for framing. The elements used as a compositional frame—trees, stairs, and other elements of entourage—can also add scale and create depth (3).

Emphasis can be given to a new structure by framing it within an existing setting, such as a historic neighboring building (4) or group of buildings.

The many considerations a photographer must resolve when he takes a picture of the completed building can give you a clue in creating new aspects of composition. Your task will be easier since you can select and eliminate objects that might interfere with your drawing.

1

2

3 4

Shades and Shadows

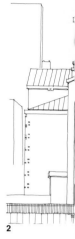

2

Linear perspective is a conventional way of representing three-dimensional objects on a flat plane. In actuality buildings and other objects never exist merely as linear outlines. We always see them as surfaces. Some are transparent, some opaque, but all are differentiated by varying tones. A photograph will record all forms by their relative values on a scale of tones ranging from black to white. These tones will appear different as the intensity and direction of light changes. Textures which appear smooth in flat lighting might become quite bold under strong crosslighting.

To study some of these changes, a series of pictures was taken of the same building at three different times of the day and from three different locations (2,6,10). The linear outlines of these three different views describe how the shapes would appear without definition of tone. The series of photographs demonstrates morning light (3,7,11), midday sun (4,8,12), and late afternoon sun (5,9,13).

6

Certain academic knowledge of plotting shadows is certainly necessary for the proper execution of a rendering. However, the selection of values in the distribution of light and shade is equally important. Often this is purely a matter of judgment. Studying photographs of actual lighting conditions on different shapes, surfaces, and materials will certainly add to that vocabulary. One of the easiest ways to accomplish this is to study photographs of buildings in periodicals. Or you might want to try your own camera on a particular case. The pictures shown here were taken with a Hasselblad fitted with a 185mm Telephoto lens at a distance of approximately 300 feet on Tri-x 120 roll film. Exposures were 1/250 second at f/16.

1

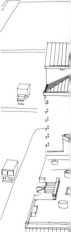

10

3

4

5

7

8

9

11

12

13

PART TWO
Preparation of the layout

Desseing d'elevation du lieu des thuilleries
sur la veue du costé du regard du Louvre

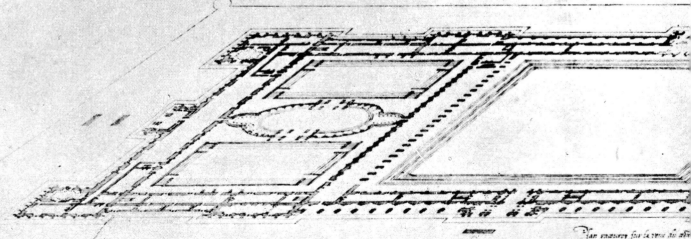

Plan mesuré sur la veue du costé
suivant le Louvre

Chapter 2

Layouts: from plans

An orthographic plan of a building is a scaled-down representation that shows how this building would appear from a viewpoint directly overhead. It is a geometrically accurate representation that describes all the proportions of the structure as it will eventually be built. If you look at this plan from any angle other than straight down, you are in effect seeing the plan in perspective. A camera would see it the same way. A photograph of this plan, taken at any oblique angle, will alter the film's representation of the plan. It will become a photographic perspective.

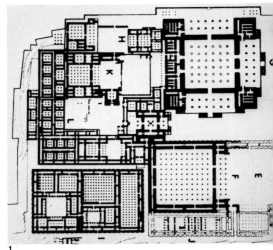

1

Photoperspectives

The delineator, whose job it is to create a perspective rendering on the basis of an orthographic plan, rarely has the opportunity to look at the plan dead on as he works from it. If he relies on the traditional methods of plotting his perspective, he will have adjusted the plan and its elevation into positions that would mechanically establish picture plane, station point, and vanishing points. But his eye is constantly seeing that plan, fixed to his working surface, in perspective. What he eventually plots, locates, and renders into a perspective drawing will actually be but one mechanical resemblance to the perspective plan his eye has seen many times and from many viewpoints.

Had the mind of that delineator the ability to freeze those impinging images into an object that he could somehow measure and scale, he would simply delineate his direct vi-

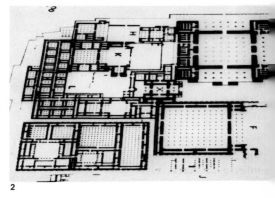

2

3

sion, unerringly, onto a new surface.

Suppose, on the other hand, that a camera had been placed at the delineator's point of view. Just as its system duplicates the physiological mechanism of the eye, so its "vision" would duplicate the delineator's vision. The plan, after all, is an object in depth when seen from an oblique angle. As previously described, the camera has the remarkable ability to create the illusion of depth of objects in space; consequently, a photograph of the plan from this viewpoint would record every subtle convergence, angularity, foreshortening of line, and diminution of scale with the same correctness as the delineator's mental vision.

In short, once the viewpoint toward the plan had been established, every existing line of it would become automatically and accurately "plotted" by aiming the camera and pushing the shutter release.

The photographed image of the plan in accurate perspective—or the "photoperspective" as it will be referred to hereafter—has abundant potential on a small piece of film. The area of importance chosen to be rendered can be selected and limited by circumscribing that area directly on the film surface. This "cropped" area can then be enlarged to the desired size of the finished drawing. The scale of the enlarged photoperspective can be determined easily by measuring some horizontal line in it and comparing its length to that same line on the original plan. Another method is to include an actual scale, like an architect's ruler, in the photo. Vanishing points can be found by tracing to convergence once parallel lines, and the horizon can be established by connecting the vanishing points with a straight line.

Capturing all this potential information on film is not a difficult chore, nor does it require the extensive technical knowledge of a professional photographer. The projects in this chapter were chosen in an effort to describe all the procedures a renderer needs to follow to make the concept of photographic perspective not only easy to use but rewarding to apply.

4

Elks Lodge

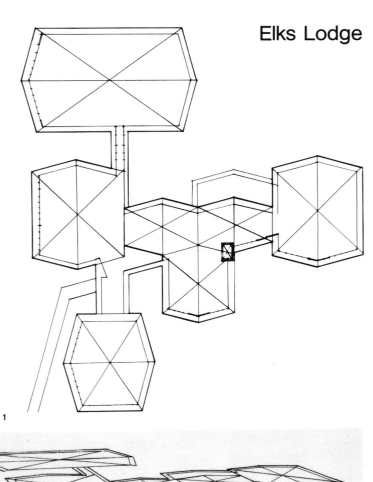

1

2

This project marks a good beginning to the practical application of photoperspective. It shows how to correct a common error experienced by those attempting the method for the first time: incorrect choice of the station point of the camera.

First the plan (1) was laid out on a drafting table and evenly illuminated with two photofloods. A reflex-type camera, on a tripod, was positioned low and oblique to the plan, far enough away from the table so that the entire plan was visible well within the limits of a normal angle of vision. Then several photos were taken, varing lengths of exposure. The resultant negative showing the best focus and contrast between plan lines and the paper was used to blow up the image to the size of the final rendering (2).

Next, a careful tracing transcribed each line of the photoperspective onto a working surface. Vanishing points were quickly located by following back once parallel lines to the place where they converged. The corners of the floor plan determined where vertical lines would establish walls. Similarly fixed by the plan was the perspective relationship between the walls and what would be the center lines of each unit (3).

Scale had been "programmed" into the photoperspective by laying an architect's ruler on the plan before it was photographed; the scale on the bottom edge of the ruler corresponded to the scale used in the original plan. Now every line of the photoperspective falling in the same plane as that of the ruler could be measured directly, using the reduced scale that was visually indicated. Consequently, at every point where the photoperspective coincided with the plane fixed by the ruler, vertical lines were drawn to their proper heights, and—using the vanishing points—enough of the remaining vertical heights were projected in and out of this plane to rough in the walls, ceiling lines, and

4

3

5

roof peak of one unit. It was immediately apparent at this stage that the station point selected was too high. Wall heights were so obscured by roof overhang that little meaningful detail could be rendered on them.

It was obvious that the view would have to be lowered; and since no alternative viewpoint had been photographed, lowering would have to be achieved using the photoperspective at hand.

An overlay was placed upon the first drawing. At every conjunctive point of the original perspective, vertical lines were projected upward and beyond the area chosen to locate the new perspective plan. Since the changes here involved only height—not nearness

of station point—the same vanishing points would work in the new perspective. Consequently all measurements and scales determined on the first perspective would be applicable to the second (4).

Using the vanishing points, the remaining lines were relocated wherever their vertical projections were intersected by lines emanating from the vanishing points. The result was a more pronounced foreshortening of the perspective plan, but the new wall heights that were determined held a more prominent relationship to the previously dominating roofs.

This second perspective plan was successfully developed to completion for the final rendering (5).

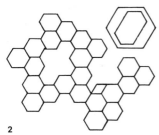

1

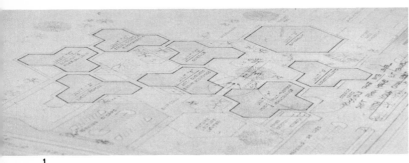

2

West
High School

The orthographic plan (2) of this high school reveals an arrangement of geometric shapes that appears difficult to plot using conventional methods. The photoperspective, on the other hand, makes it look relatively easy. The shapes of all the units, in perspective, were plotted simultaneously by the camera (1).

Many photographs had been taken, to determine the best possible relationship of forms and the most pleasing composition. The picture chosen for enlargement had two sides of the six-sided figure parallel to the picture plane (3). This left two other pairs of sides for which vanishing points had to be plotted. Vanishing point right was located on the drafting table. Vanishing point left, however, was so remote that diminution toward it was practically nonexistent. As a result, all lines receding to it were traced as parallels. Working with this plan led to a reevaluation of some of the techniques normally employed in creating a perspective drawing. Were vanishing points really necessary?

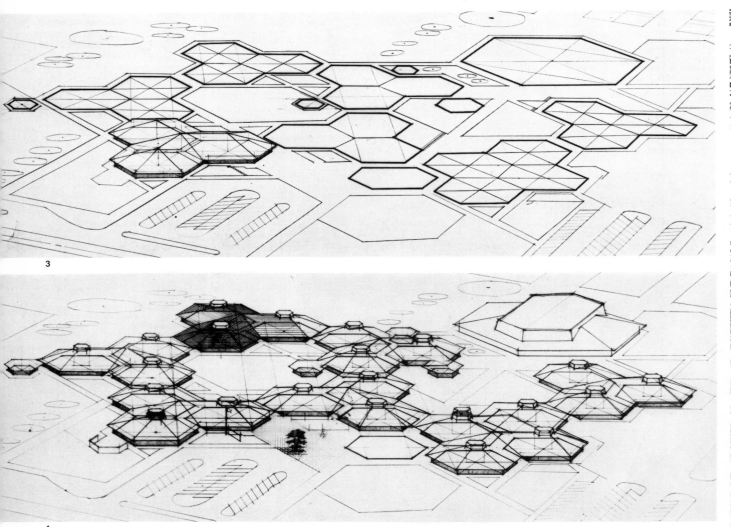

3

4

5

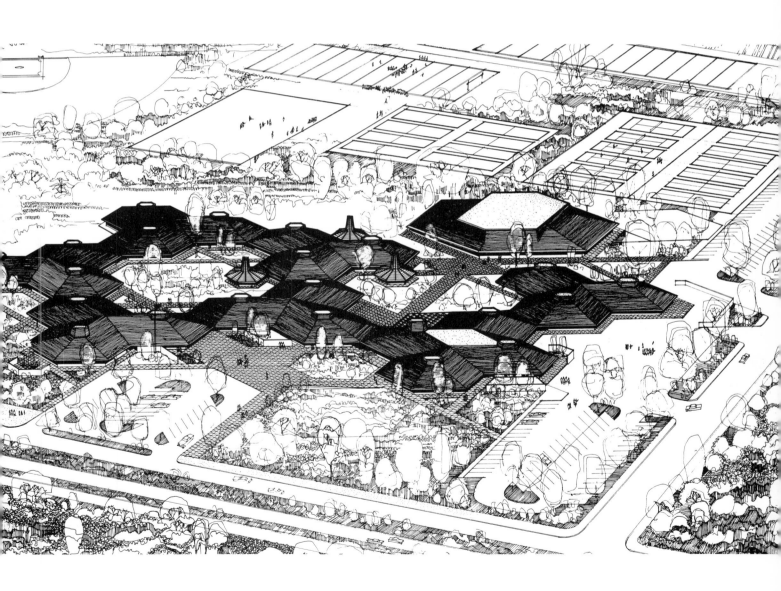

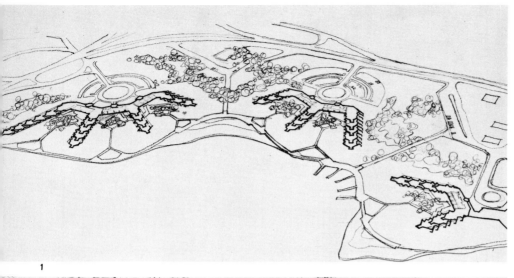

1

Some structures are complex not only in plan, but equally in elevation. With the photoperspective (1) of the plan the verticals can be projected to whatever height necessary (2).

First each exposed side of the structure is built up floor by floor much like an isometric drawing (4). Diminution and convergence are negligible, due to the distant vanishing points. Next, the balconies are projected from each of these floor lines and windows added where necessary (3, 5). If handled in this fashion, the whole (7) will not be any more difficult than the sum of its parts.

6

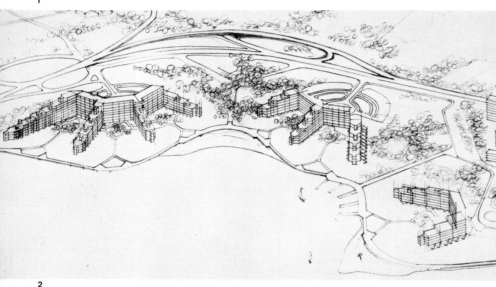

2

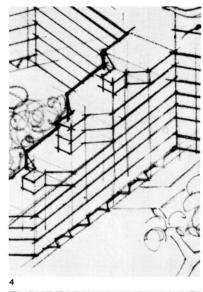

4

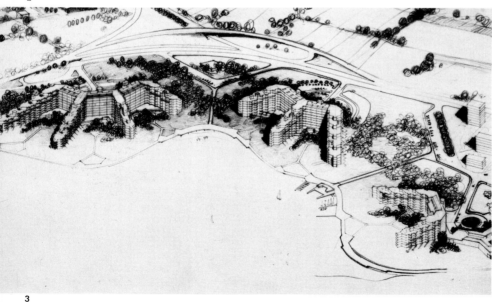

3

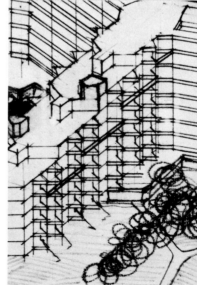

5

7

Offenburg

1

Camelback Inn

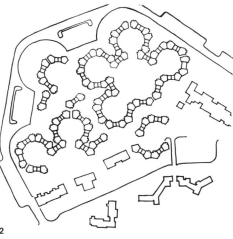

2

This organic arrangement of pentagonally shaped units would have given the most experienced layout draftsman a difficult time. No aspect of the plan could be called a frontal or a lateral view (2). The problem was to determine an aesthetic balance of the masses without destroying the plasticity created by the linking of the units. This difficult problem was also solved simply by the photoperspective (1).

Several pictures of the plan were taken from different angles and varying heights. The compositionally "right" (3) view was almost immediately apparent. The negative selected was placed in a mount and the image was enlarged to the desired size, using an ordinary slide projector. The plan was projected onto a piece of paper taped to the studio wall, and the outlines of the plan were traced in pencil onto the paper. This tracing became the basis for the perspective drawing.

Each pentagonal unit was turned slightly from its neighbor so that vanishing points were totally useless. Therefore, each unit was treated as a separate drawing and linked together to create the total picture (6).

4

5

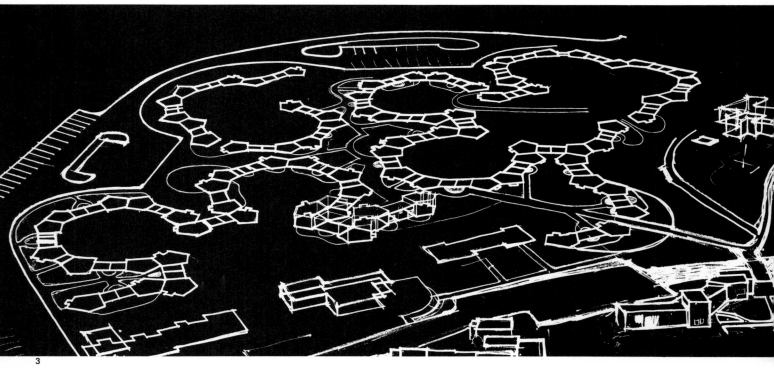

3

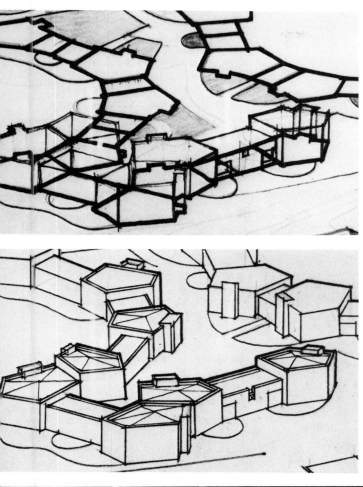

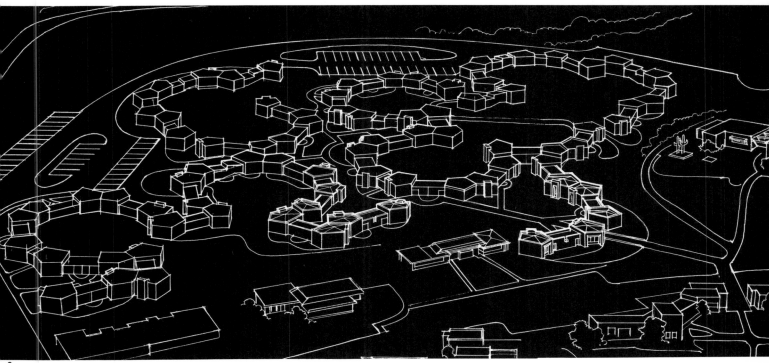

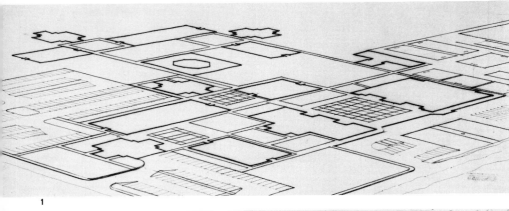

1

Vanden High School

A rectilinear plan naturally lends itself to establishing certain guidelines for the execution of a layout (1). The plan itself, as seen in the photoperspective, is already a perspective grid. Therefore, any line added to that plan can be placed there, using the existing lines as a guide (2). From this simple beginning an entire rendering can be constructed without the use of vanishing points (3,4).

Care must be exercised in photographing the plan to ensure that background forms are not obscured by those in the foreground. This can be overcome by taking several pictures using an elevated tripod.

After a vertical scale has been established on the photoperspective, all vertical elements can be projected up from their point in plan. Then the roof configuration of each structure can be roughly sketched in. Next an accurate layout is made over this rough outline and the location of trees added before commencing with the final ink rendering (5).

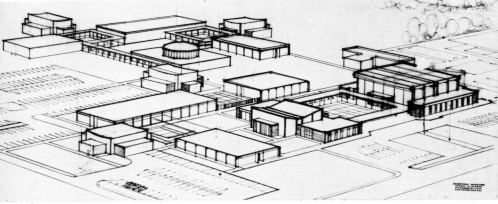

2

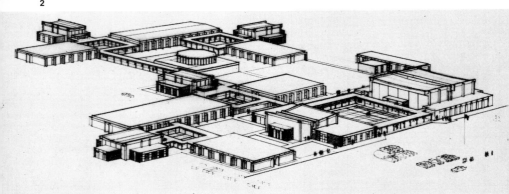

3

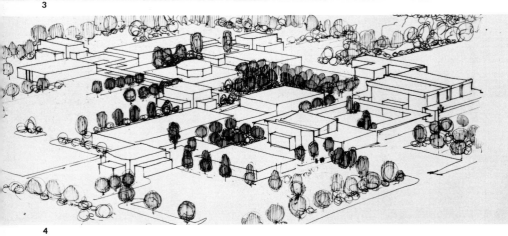

4

5

The Custom Grid

The basic tool of the photoperspective is the custom grid. It is not a perspective grid in the common sense of the word, since it does not "diminish" as other grids do. Diminishing is "built in" to the photograph of the plan in perspective, and the grid will also be in perspective. Rather than a grid on which measurements can be taken, it is simply a guide for converging lines in one, two, or any number of directions.

Vertical heights can be scaled on any portion of the plan by simply selecting a line in a position parallel to the picture plane and measuring it against the same line on the actual plan. A ratio will thereby be established between the actual line *AB* on the photoperspective and the one on the drawing *AB*. Any height can then be found easily at that point. If any known height at the foremost portion of the grid is traced back, following the converging grid lines, it will be the correct height anywhere in the perspective. If this same line were traced back to the point of origin, it would enclose a geometric shape.

To establish the grid, simply take any two originally parallel lines from the photoperspective (1), preferably the nearest and the most distant, and extend them to each edge of the drawing on the left. You now have a trapezoidal shape (*ABCD*) with one side shorter than the other. Select a scale such as $\frac{1}{8}'' = 1'0''$, and place the scale vertically to the horizon. Mark equal division between *A* and *B*. On the right side select a scale slightly larger, such as $\frac{1}{4}'' = 1'0''$, and place the scale in such a manner that you arrive at the same number of divisions between *C* and *D* as on the left side. Now connect point for point each corresponding number (2,3). This grid shows the perspective convergence to the left vanishing point. The same procedure will establish a converging grid for the right vanishing point. You now have a custom grid—tailored to your photoperspective—and from that grid you can determine the convergence of each and every line of your drawing.

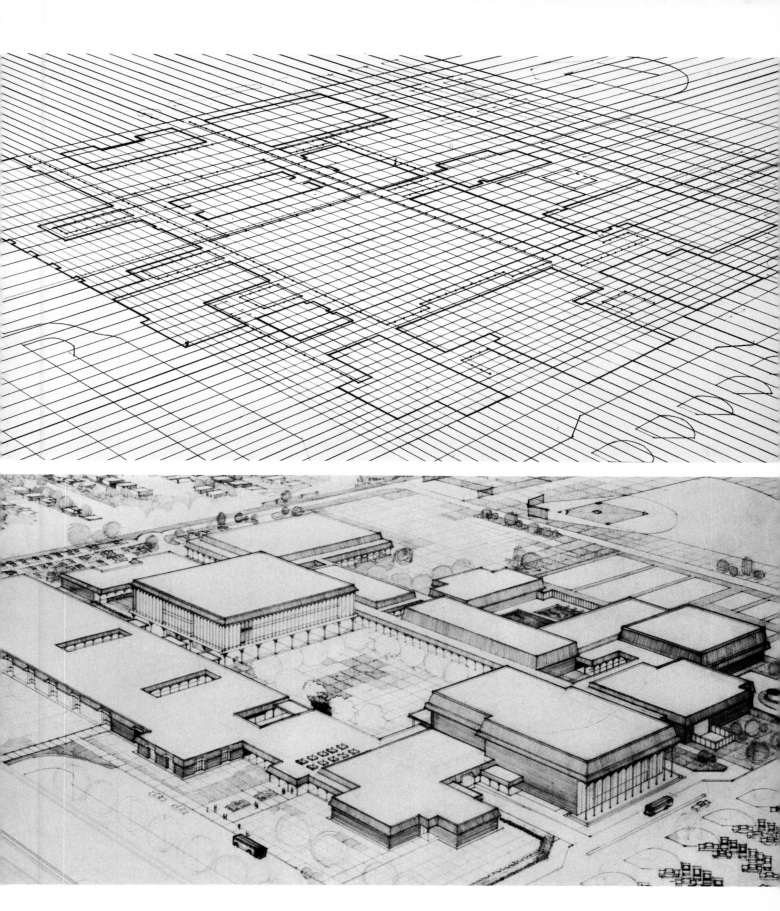

1

2

Rosewood Estates

Some plans may contain a combination of forms, some of which may be easy to project up from the photo-perspective, and others which are relatively simple in plan but complex in elevation.

To overcome this, you can combine a semi-stage set model with the plan, as was done for this project (1). The elevations were pasted onto cardboard and put up as props, leaving the rest of the plan on a flat plane.

Since the elevation represents projections on a flat plane, the cardboard stage set represents only that one plane. The balconies which extend from that plane had to be projected out. The actual distance was determined by proportioning (2).

The small housing units flanking the larger structure were simply projected up from the plan, using methods previously described (3, 4)

3

4

1

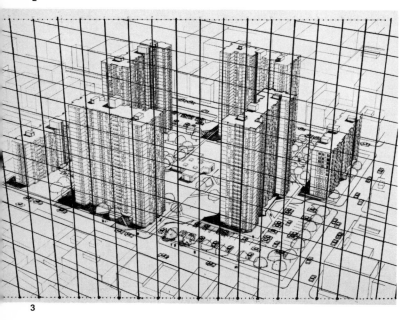

2

3

Low-cost Housing Project

One would not expect so much information to be contained on a single piece of film. However, the photo (1) here contains all the information necessary to complete the rendering. In addition, the entire drawing was done without a T square or conventional vanishing points.

First a vertical scale was essential, but if a solid stage set model were built, as in the preceding example, the structures in front would obscure the structures in the rear. It was decided to simply indicate floor heights on strips of cardboard, which would ultimately be represented as precast concrete panel joints, and prop them up vertically at each of the four corners of the structure. This allowed the plan to show through (2), and very little detail was covered up.

The angle of view and the high station point necessitated a three-point perspective, which ordinarily would be mechanical nightmare. Here a third custom grid was added to the other two to accommodate the third vanishing point (3). This eliminated the use of a T square for the verticals. You, therefore, have a layout done totally without conventional mechanical aid and one which is totally visually correct in every way. All the information necessary for the completion of the drawing was contained on one piece of film—the photograph of the plan.

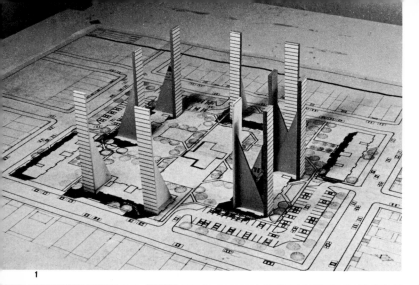

4

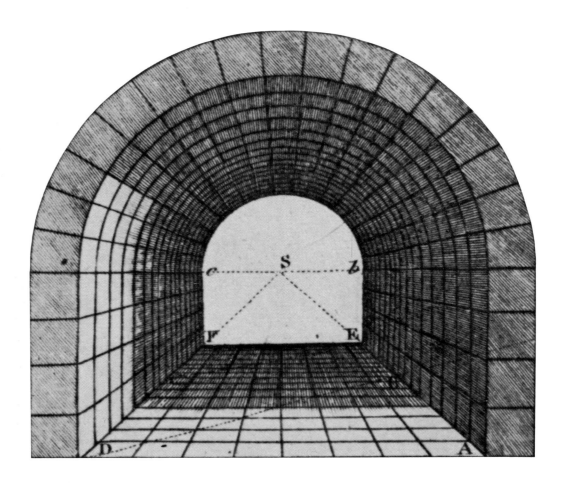

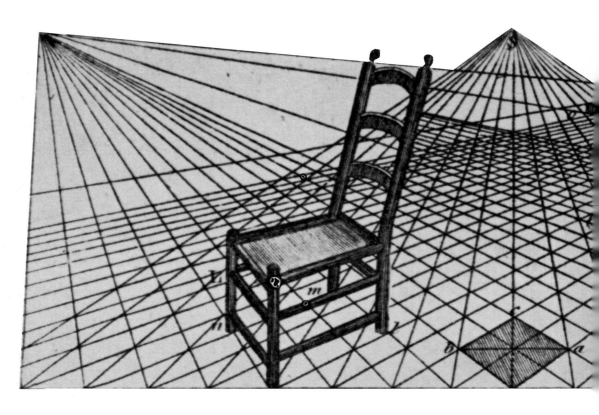

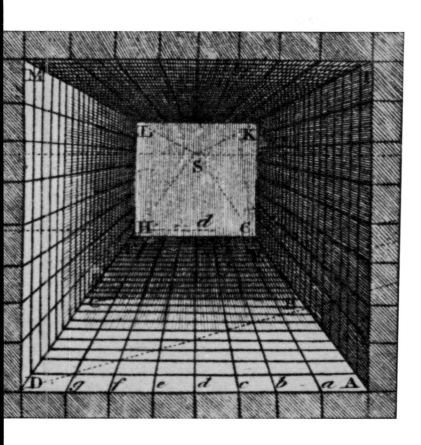

Chapter 3

Layouts: from models

Models can be classified in three major ways: models for (1) photography, (2) study, and (3) presentation. This chapter deals only with models for photography. They are inexpensive, simple to build, and disposable. The model for the camera need only be built where the camera will see it. The benefits of the photographic approach are many, but they diminish if the proper attitude toward models is not considered. They are simply aids to drawing perspective and have no value in themselves. They must be considered dispensable once they have been photographed. If they are good enough to keep around, they were too good for the purpose.

Types of Models

Stage Set—Type 1

The simplest of models can be constructed from the architectural drawings, preliminaries, or sketches. These drawings are simply pasted on cardboard and set up like props. This model is built only where the camera will see it, which can usually be determined beforehand. The cardboard model represents only one plane of the structure, which is perfectly adequate for most projects.

5

Stage Set—Type 2

Similar to the type 1 stage set in that the elevations are pasted on cardboard, it differs in that additional elements can be added to create depth. Roof overhangs can be added as well as projections of any kind. Scale figures and scale automobiles can also assist in getting a more realistic preview of what the drawing will be like.

Structural Cardboard

Usually employed when it is desirable to see into a structure, this model is much more complex to build. Contours are easy to build out of cardboard, provided the scale is correct. Models of this type are even less difficult to build out of Styrofoam core board.

Interior Model

This is truly a stage set in every sense of the word. It can be built with or without ceilings, and usually three interior walls are advisable. If there are columns or obstructions in the room, it is a good idea to put them into the model. They can be quite a distraction if they are not placed properly.

9

Contour Model

The model for land shapes can be made easily by utilizing cardboard for the contours as opposed to the expensive machine-milled Styrofoam contours associated with presentation models. Visually, this type of model is best suited for slide presentation use, as it is too elaborate for rendering purposes.

6

Box Model

A simple stage set model is carried to completion, by constructing all sides and enclosing it. This adds a solidity to the model and is more reliable for larger buildings where true vertical is desired. The main advantage is that any number of views can be taken from any angle, since it is a complete model. However, it should be constructed without an investment of time, since it will probably be disposed of.

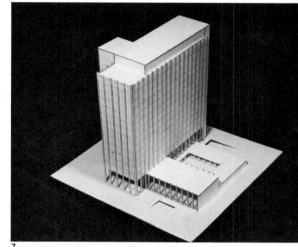

7

Mass Model

This is similar to the box model in that it is complete in three dimensions. When shapes are too complex to build from cardboard, a solid form is easier to use. Again, the elevations are pasted over this form. The mass model, because of its solidity, tends to be more accurate than the cardboard, and corners and uprights tend to be true.

Presentation Model

Used primarily for slide and film presentations, it must be well built but is still not in the class of models built by professional model makers.

8

1

2

San Angelo Mall

Frequently you may want to do sketches of a preliminary concept which has not yet been designed. This is possible using the simplest of model-building techniques, the stage set model.

Draw your design requirements to some convenient scale. If the buildings have not yet been designed, simply draw floor-to-floor heights and some convenient bay spacing. Or you may want to just indicate the bulk of the structure without detail. These simple drawings can then be pasted on cardboard and set up in place on an impromptu plot plan. Use simple materials to create a sense of scale, such as toy cars, cotton balls for trees, and flat head screws for light standards. Take several pictures of each scene, mostly at eye level. These can then be quickly developed into environmental sketches. If the arrangement in plan is accurate, you will have sketches that are easy to produce, and they will have more credibility than a drawing executed over a thumbnail sketch.

The drawings shown here were all executed directly over an enlargement of the stage set model, without an intermediate layout stage. Using an acetate overlay for the drawing is the easiest method of translating the information on the picture to the basis for a drawing.

5

6

3

4

1

2

The simple stage set model can be extremely flexible in application. Here two drawings of an interior square were required: one from ground level (1), and a second from an office window above the roof of the square (5). The same model was used for both views. The model consisted of two walls and a plot plan.

In the ground-level view (3), an office building was added in the background, using scaled heights

4

Lancaster Square

3

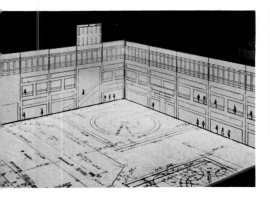

5

taken from the model photograph. The second view (4) was a low aerial view looking down from this office building into the square. Here the plot plan was of great assistance.

In the lower view, certain foreground elements were added to create a sense of depth and scale (2). In the second view the interior of an office was added to frame the drawing and give it the proper sense of height (6).

6

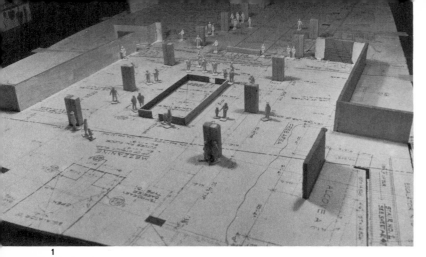

1

2

B.A.R.T. Station

Models of large interior spaces with normal ceiling heights are difficult to photograph when built to a scale smaller than ½ inch to the foot. Another problem that occurs with interior spaces is the difficulty in lighting the space. One solution to both of these problems is to leave the ceiling off the model, but show columns or other objects in their correct position and correct height (1).

When photographing the interior model, be sure to place the camera at the proper eye level. To accomplish this, set the model on a table top and place the camera at the front edge of the table. To get closer views, move the model closer to the table edge. If the camera were placed on the table itself, the center of the lens would measure higher than eye level (2).

One way to visualize the proper eye level when viewing the model through the camera lens is to place scale figures inside the model at various locations. By this method of previewing the scene beforehand it was discovered that the vastness of the station did not permit detail to be shown. Therefore, several views were taken, each one successively closer, by moving the model closer to the camera at the table edge (3).

The final selection was a view which was so close to a stairway opening that it would also disclose a view of the lower-level train platform (4).

3

VIEW #5

4

1

IBM Cafeteria

Whenever the ceiling of an interior space is an important feature in the drawing, it should be included in the model. The scale of the model should be at least ½ inch to the foot.

The ceiling pattern was created by drawing one typical bay to scale and photocopying it 18 times to make up the entire ceiling pattern (5).

Since the ceiling was more than 12 inches from the floor, lighting was not a problem. The camera had to be placed outside the model to obtain the proper eye level. Toy figures were placed at random inside the model to give a sense of scale to the interior space (1). After the photograph was enlarged to the desired size, two overlays were made on acetate. The first one completed the arrangement of figures and furniture (2), and the second completed the ceiling pattern (3). One of the unique advantages of this particular model was using it to create two renderings: the first of the cafeteria and a second of the lobby area immediately adjacent to it. Since the structural ceiling was the same for both areas, the only thing needed for the lobby view was two walls. The ceiling was reused (6,7).

5

2

3

4

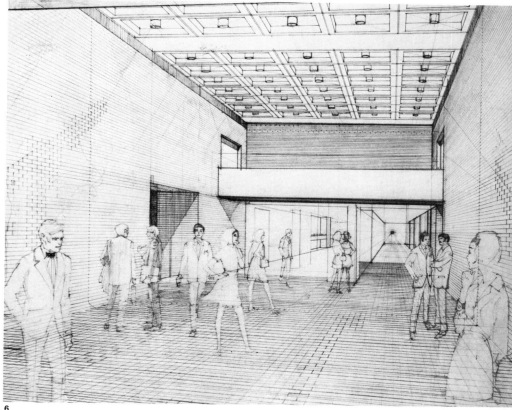

6

7

Law Office Building

There may be times when it is desirable to preview your rendering while it is still in the model stage. Adding certain elements to the model can facilitate this. Plastic molded toy figures and scale automobiles parked in their proper location give this model photograph a sense of realism (1).

Certain simple projections like roof overhangs are easily applied when building the model and eliminate the work required to project them to the proper location in the layout (2).

The pencil overlay was done to establish the range of values for the drawing before it was executed in ink. From start to finish very little changed from the scene established originally in the photograph of the model (3).

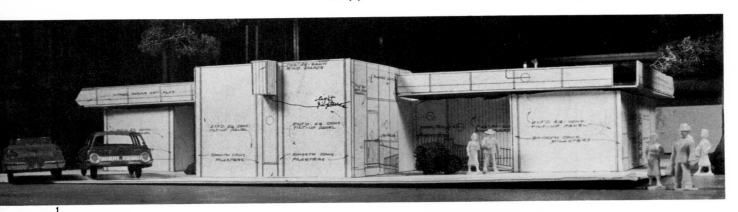

1

2

3

1

2

Williamsville Offices

Whenever a major portion of any design contains a large transparent area, it is most desirable to build it as a transparent wall. This means that whatever walls or forms would show on the inside should be constructed along with the model (1,2).

The transparent wall can be made of glass, plastic, or acetate, depending on the need for strength, the method of construction, and the size of the area. The obvious benefit of the transparent wall is that all the relationships between the outside of the structure and the interior are plainly visible in the viewer of the camera. If the window areas are small and are not going to be predominantly transparent, then a simple outline of the window area on the wall of the model will suffice (3).

If you have access only to an early study model which is complete except for design revisions, you can still make good use of it. If pictures of this model are combined with those of a stage set model, certain benefits can be realized. For example, the correct placement of trees and exact positioning of playground

4

3

Washington Heights

5

equipment was taken from the site study model (4). The window treatment, which had been revised since the earlier model was built, was taken from a stage set model (5). The two models were photographed from exactly the same angle, distance, and eye level, making it possible to select the details desired from both models for inclusion in the layout (6). Figures were added to the layouts later and were kept casual in dress, posture, and movement. This helped to create a relaxed neighborhood atmosphere (7).

6

7

1

Bethel A.M.E. Church

Here the free form of the structure is best expressed by the architect's own study model built of balsa wood (1). This simulated the actual building material: precast concrete ribs tied together with sprayed concrete. More than 36 photos were taken of this model, all from ground level, in order to study the subtle change of form as one moved around the structure. The view chosen showed each of the two entrances and was therefore the most desirable (2).

A pencil study was made first from a direct projection of the negative onto tracing paper. Then a careful ink drawing was executed over the pencil rough, still retaining the ribbed aspect of the initial model (3).

2

3

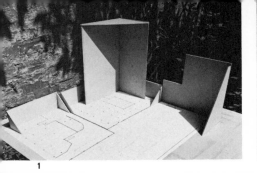

1

2

3

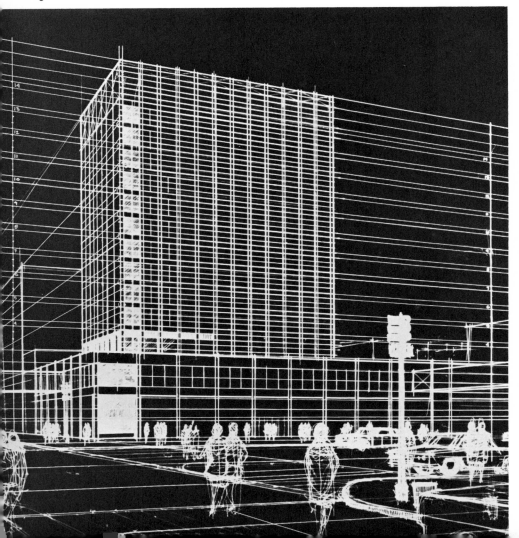

American National Bank

There is little need to build the areas of the model which the camera will not see. Once you have decided on the possible viewpoints, you should build the model to satisfy only those conditions (1,2).

For this project the elevations were drawn on tracing paper with a heavy ink line to indicate floor heights and window divisions. This paper was pasted onto cardboard, cut out, and assembled into a simple stage set model (3). Props were used behind the façade to keep each side upright, and the corners were reinforced with a triangular cardboard piece to ensure right angles.

The model was then taken outdoors for photographing, as photofloods were not available at the time. This provided very even illumination on the sunny side of the building but tended to obscure the detail on the shady side. However, the detail was sufficiently clear upon enlargement to use the negative.

When one of the vanishing points is off the board, you can construct a grid to give you the proper convergence. On the right-hand side of the drawing, construct a vertical line and mark off equal increments on the ¼-inch scale between points A and B. Next, take this same number of increments on the ⅜-inch scale and move the scale, held vertically, back and forth until the same number falls between A and B. Then connect each corresponding number on the two scales. This will give you the true perspective convergence to a distant vanishing point on the right (4).

4

5

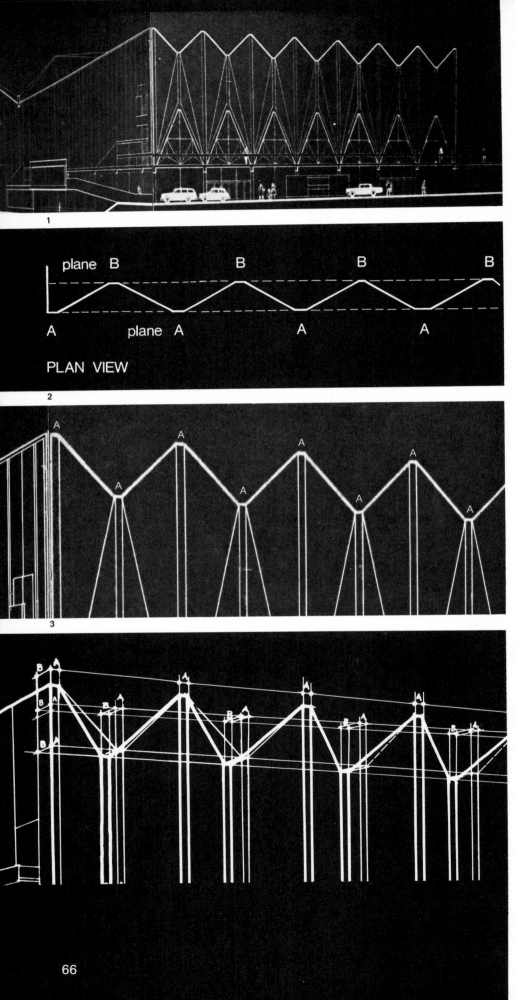

1

plane B   B   B   B

A   plane A   A   A

PLAN VIEW

2

3

4

5

7

Civic Auditorium

When drawn in plan and elevation view, most structures can be described by certain fixed planes. These planes are easy to represent by utilizing simple cardboard forms. More complicated structures, however, require certain adjustments in order to make full use of the photographic technique (1).

You could spend a little additional time building the model to conform more closely to an irregular shape. You might find it easier, however, to consider everything as being projected onto a flat plane, such as the elevations, and build a simple model representing those planes. After the picture is enlarged, you can project objects in front of, or in back of, these preselected planes.

After the plans and elevations for the coliseum shown here were studied, it was decided that the simple model would supply information for the layout. The front façade of the building was, in plan view, much like the pleats of an accordian or camera bellows. In elevation, of course, the pleats were all flattened onto the same plane. This meant that certain lines that were not in that plane would have to be located by other means.

The plane of the front façade is denoted by the letter A. The inside plane is denoted by the letter B. To find plane B in the photograph, you simply measure its distance back in plan view (2). Call this distance X. By projecting plane B in plan view to the outside wall, you can determine exactly where it falls in elevation. Mark this on the enlarged photograph of the model (3,4).

The peaks of A remain where they are in the photograph since they are in the plane of the model. The valleys must be projected back to plane B as shown in (3). With this established, the rest of the layout will fall right into place (5,6).

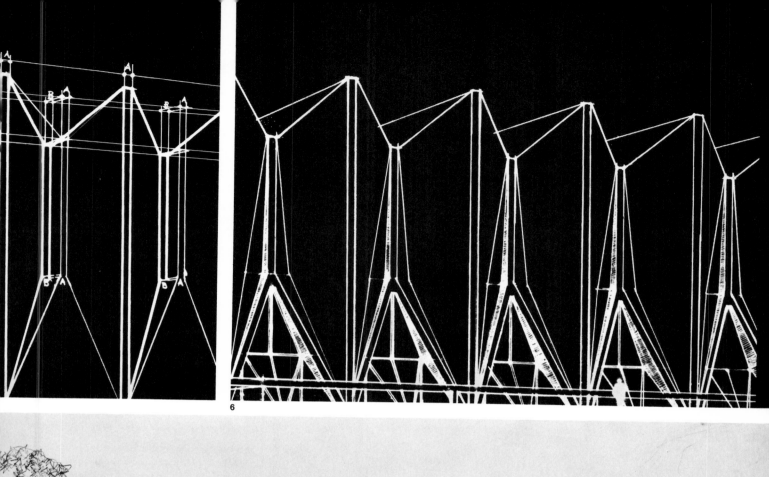

6

Two Firehouses

1

2

3

4

5

6

San Francisco

Berkeley

The more complete a model is, the greater the advantage in using it to prepare a layout. If a model has been built for another purpose, you can still use it for your perspective.

In the two examples here the architects had already built study models, both of structural cardboard so that you could see into them.

In the San Francisco firehouse the interior of the structure was clearly visible from a low viewpoint. This is a little more elaborate than what is usually required to do a perspective. Some information was taken from the plans and elevations, but mostly from the model (1,2,3).

In the Berkeley firehouse project the model was not as carefully constructed, yet all the essential elements were there. It is quite an easy matter to straighten up the various planes on the pencil layout and to locate the vanishing points at that time. Any revisions to the drawing can be easily and quickly made at this point using the information available from the model photo. The major benefit to the cardboard model is that it provides more information than the single-plane, stage set model (4,5,6).

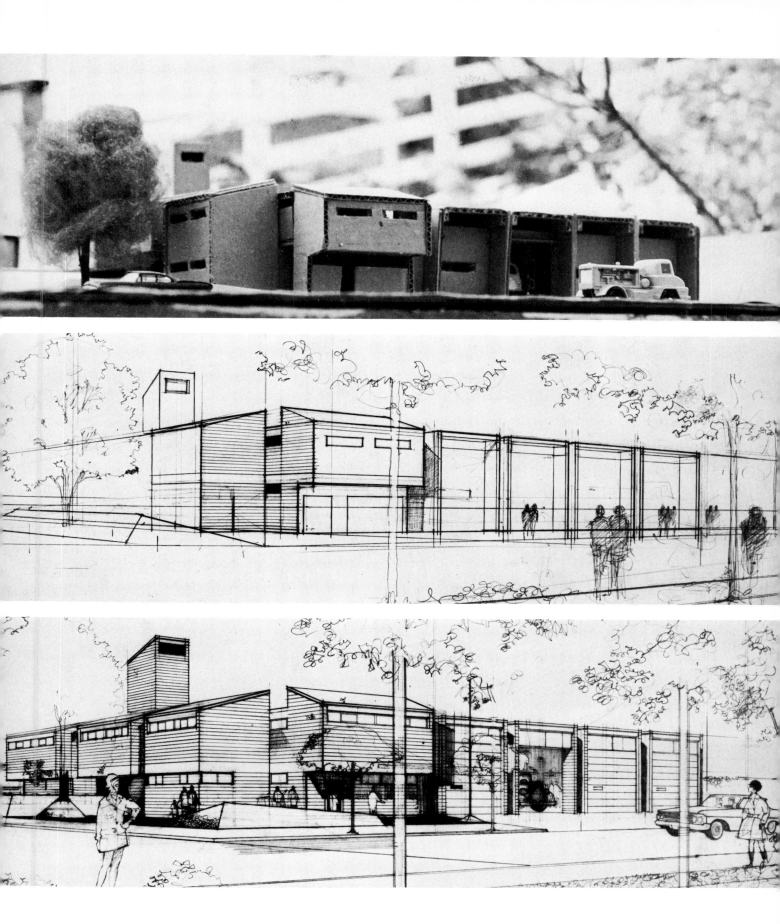

1

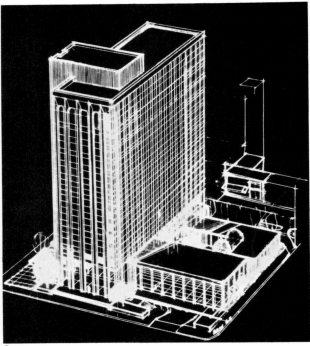

2

Bank of California

The intended use of a model should dictate the extent and quality of the construction. If a model is to be seen from only one side, it should not be necessary to build the rest of the model. When several views are required, however, a box model may be more appropriate (1).

The box model is enclosed on all sides and is generally hollow. This complete enclosure adds strength and stability to the model.

For this project, a box model was used to provide views from two viewpoints. One view was photographed in such a manner that it could be used in an aerial layout. Two ground-level views of the model were also produced, focusing on two different sides of the structure.

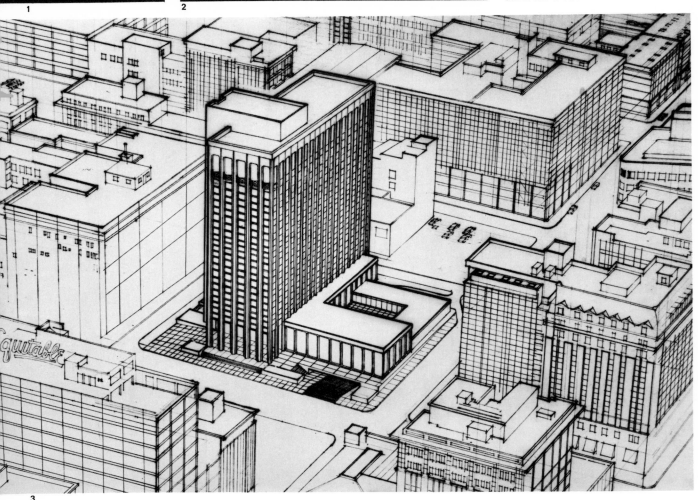

3

4

5

6

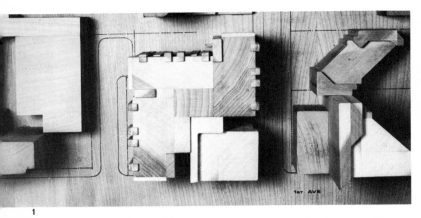

1

2

Dental College

Many times an architect will have a mass model made for design study purposes. These models will be of some value in determining a view-point to use, but they usually contain only general information. This information is usually not sufficient to produce a layout (1,2,3).

On the other hand, you can construct a mass model yourself very easily. You will enjoy the advantages of true corners and plumb walls not always inherent in the stage set type of model.

By scaling a floor plan to standard balsa wood sizes, you can construct the model very easily. Using rubber cement as an adhesive, coat both pieces and put them together while very wet. You will find that the pieces can be moved for quite some time while the parts are properly aligned. The elevations can then be pasted onto the sides. It is usually easiest to do this last and then make what-ever minor adjustments in thickness are necessary (4,5,6).

With this model you can now get any number of accurate views (7,8).

5

3

4

Bunker Hill Towers

Naturally, the more complete the model, the easier it is to create perspective renderings from it. With such a complete model as the one shown here, many different approaches are possible. Several views were taken in order to study the relationship of the lower pyramidal structures to the towers in the background. In photographing such a model, you may introduce a third vanishing point by tilting the camera if you do not have perspective controls on it. However, this can be easily corrected on the drawing board by choosing a plane at the horizon line and using the dimensions at that line, make all the verticals straight. For additional guidance you can establish a custom grid over the elevations.

1

2
3

4

5

6

1

2

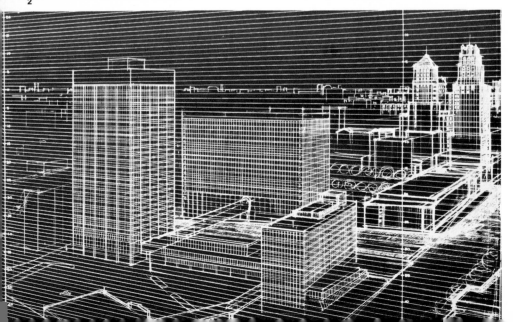

3

Gateway

The model is a valuable tool for the perspective artist, but certain precautions should be taken when photographing a group of stage set models. These are not as accurate as more elaborate models and are sometimes difficult to align properly. When arranging a group of buildings on the plot plan, it is hard to judge by eye how accurately they are placed. Even a slight error can be bothersome when enlarged.

To compensate for this, a custom grid is used to ensure that everything in the drawing will converge in the same plane. It is much easier to correct the alignment on the drawing board than it is to worry about perfect placement of the elements on the plot plan.

In this case, photographs of two separate models were combined to produce the final layout. The one used to obtain information for the background was the architect's early study model. The stage set model represented the latest design of the structures and was constructed in the studio. The two negatives were then enlarged by projecting them onto the same piece of paper, to the same size and to the same scale. Then the grid was drawn over the entire drawing to make certain that the background buildings and the project structures were in alignment. After this was accomplished, the drawing was carried to completion.

4

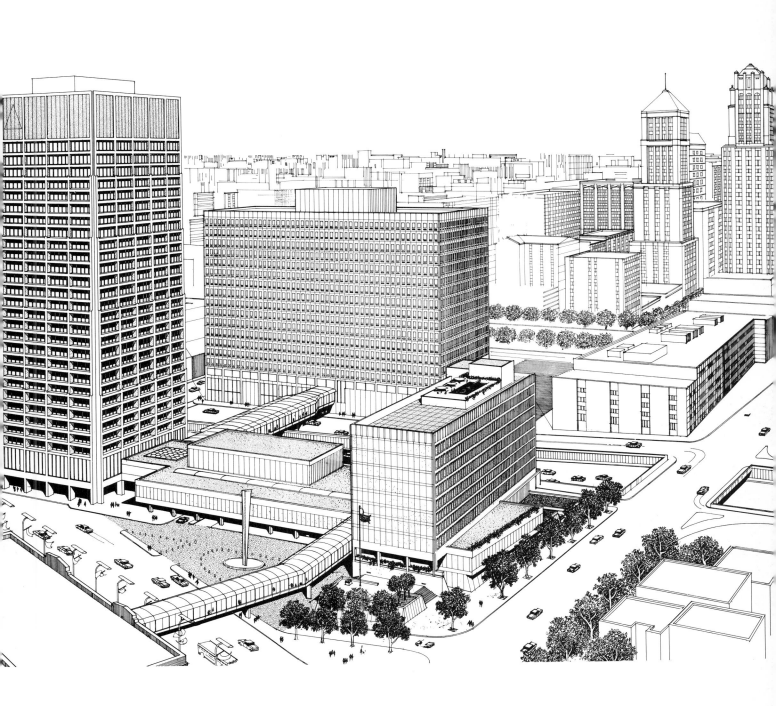

1

Gateway

Cardboard study models often serve more purposes than they were originally intended for. If such a model exists, you can use it to advantage even if it does not contain all the detail you would like. Lacking from the model shown here (1) were lines marking the horizontal division of the walls of the long low hotel unit in the foreground into precast units. The floor levels were indicated in the rough model. To find the panel divisions horizontally was relatively simple. A vertical line was drawn at the corner of the building and, using a convenient scale, the exact number of horizontal divisions were marked off along the vertical line *AB* beginning at the point labeled zero (which could have been located anywhere convenient on *AB*). Next a line labeled *C* was located at the opposite end of the structure representing the end of the divisions.

There were 54 divisions in the length of the elevation. This was broken down into 9 major divisions and 6 minor divisions within each 9. These were laid off vertically at the near edge of the building represented by the line *AB*. Then each division was projected toward the vanishing point on the right side. Since this was off the board, a custom grid served the same purpose. Then a diagonal was drawn from *B* to *C*. The intersections of this diagonal with the 54 divisions going toward the vanishing point gave the perspective diminishing dimension to each panel unit. All that was required then was to drop each intersection perpendicularly down to the surface to be divided.

2

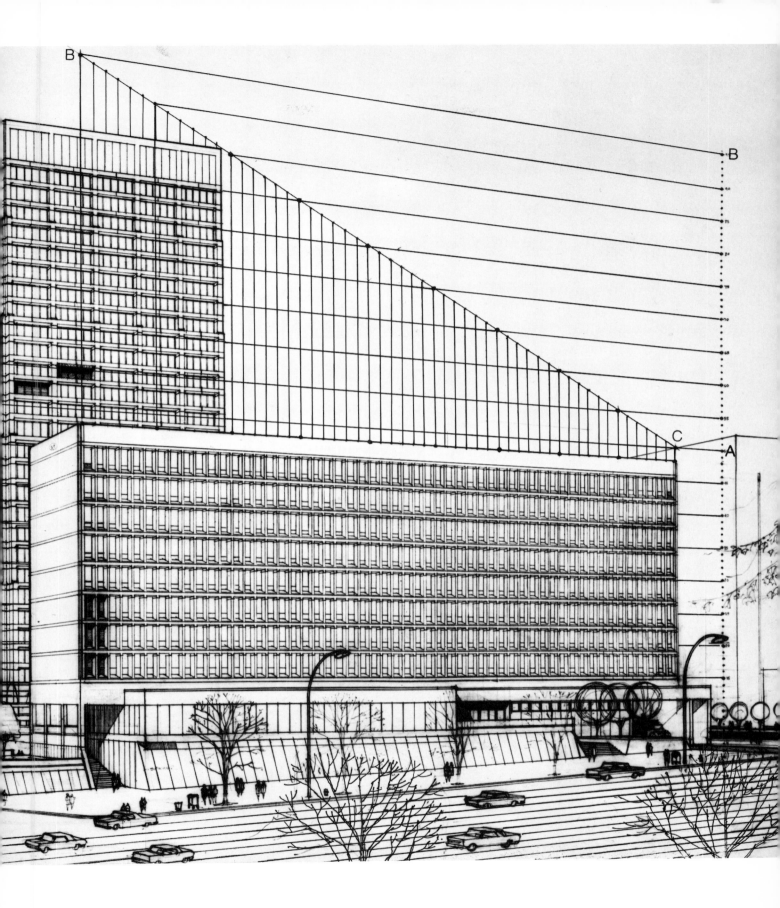

1

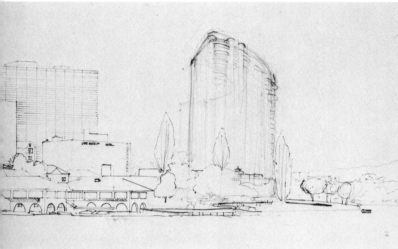

2

Lake Merrit Apartments

If you already have a model built for study purposes, you might be tempted to see how your new project will fit into the environment. So without any elaborate preparations you might go to the site and take a few site photos and, by approximating the same conditions in the office, take a few shots of your model. By enlarging the site negative to the desired size of your rendering and enlarging a photo of the model to the same size, you can see at a glance whether or not this is the best viewpoint (1,2).

In the case here, two things were apparent. First, the background buildings were strong design elements and dominated the drawing. If these buildings were left out, there would be no need for site considerations at all, since only the new building would show. Second, the apartment was to be located on a circular corner lot at the edge of a lake, and this relationship was not at all apparent in the view studied. The model and the site were then rephotographed from an aerial angle to show their proper relationships (3,4,5).

3

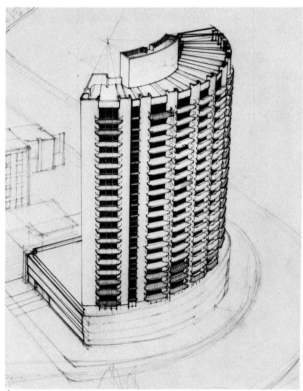

4   5

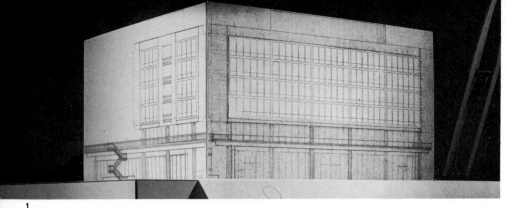

1

2

Model to Site

A rendering is like an anticipated photograph of the completed building, and if the completed project is photographed from the proper angle, it should compare well with your rendering.

In the examples here, three projects were visited after the structures were built. The results indicate the comparison that can be made.

In the first sequence, the model was a simple stage set made from two pieces of cardboard set at right angles to each other. The elevations were pasted onto the cardboard. The plane of the cardboard was the plane of the outside surface of the precast concrete window panels. Therefore, the windows, being recessed from this surface, had to be projected back a small amount.

The plaza ultimately extended to the right of the building rather than to the left as in the rendering. Other than that there is very little difference between the rendering and the completed building.

5

3

4

The third example is one where the actual site was photographed prior to executing the rendering. There was no attempt to coordinate any particular view of the existing features with the new structure. Therefore, the picture of the completed structure differs from the rendering in the positioning of the foreground tree. This was initially taken from a different position, yet added to the drawing to give depth and scale to the drawing. The following chapter describes the advantages that accrue when you visit the site with the express purpose of coordinating the site with the new project.

8

6

7

In the second comparison, the model was already available from the architect. The model was photographed from a close station point, which necessitated tilting the camera to include the top of the building. The result was a three-point perspective where the building converged toward the top. This convergence did not appear unnatural, so it was rendered this way. As the photograph of the completed structure indicates, this is exactly how the building appears from street level, and from a similar station point.

9

10

Chapter 4

Site-coordinated layouts

In architectural rendering, the delineator has specific problems of approach: representation of the three-dimensional aspects of the subject, lighting of the subject, rendition of surfaces and textures, and depiction of the immediate environment of the subject. Of these major aspects, the most important, and the most commonly overlooked, is the relationship of the subject to its environment. There is not a building in existence that benefits from the same detached simplicity as the architect's plans and elevations. Therefore, an effort to incorporate into the rendering of a structure the reality that exists around the site will be of greatest importance.

1

The Site Survey

The camera is indispensable in capturing the environment of the site. If you go to the site and shoot dozens of random photographs from various angles and distances, there is a good chance that at least some of them will be usable. However, if the site is an unfamiliar one, you should make one preliminary visit. Walk around the site and orient yourself to the environment. Considering the spread or height of the proposed structure, determine all the possible choices of station point. Decide if you want a ground-level or an aerial rendering or one that is somewhere above ground level. Then determine whether it will be possible to shoot the site from that station point or if some existing structure or object will interfere. Think about the composition of the drawing and whether or not you can use foreground elements to show a scale relationship to the proposed structure. After considering the possible station points, establish a time of day to shoot the site, determined by the angle of the sun. Flat lighting is best for survey pictures as the light produces heavy shadows that obscure detail. If this is an important factor, you can take two exposures, one for the highlights and one to record detail in the shadow area. After having made all these determinations, you are much better prepared to go to the site and obtain some meaningful site photos from the viewpoint selected. This preliminary working out also allows you to limit the equipment necessary and take only those items you will need.

If the station point selected happens to be from another building, it would be wise to obtain permission prior to going to the site. This will save making on-the-spot arrangements, which can sometimes prove bothersome. The best time to record the site would be on a weekend, when there is little traffic and less interference; however, there may not be anyone available to let you into the building. Advance planning is the key, or you might find yourself wasting much valuable time with all your photographic gear, awaiting approval to enter a building.

When you go to the site to take the pictures, be sure to take extra film in case other views occur to you. It was a lot of work to get to this point, now make use of it all.

Since a tripod is more cumbersome than it is worth in most instances, it is always a good idea to have some fast film available, like Tri-x. This allows you to take hand-held pictures in practically any lighting conditions, even rainy days. Although you would not normally take a site survey on a rainy day, there may not be any other choice. The hand-held shot is completely practical since you may be on a fire escape or balcony, or even leaning out a window. If possible, keep the camera level at all times; however, if there is minor convergence of the parallel lines, they can be straightened up in printing or on the drawing board. The main object is to record the setting in its proper scale and relationship so that your drawing of the new structure will fit into the scene.

2

1

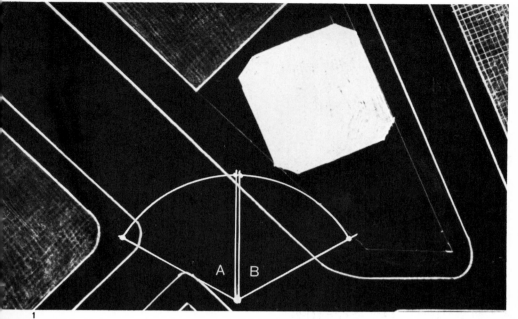

2

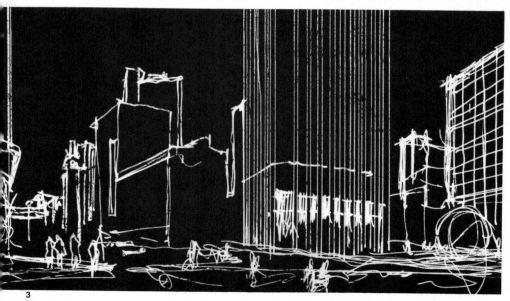

3

Crocker Plaza

Let the site photo create the important reference material: vanishing points, horizon line, and the shape of your project in perspective. Something from the site photo, such as people or light standards, can give you a clue as to the actual scale at any point, or you could make notes while on the site as to certain heights of adjacent structures by either measurements or estimation. From the site photo itself, there will be many checkpoints to give you aid in coordinating it with your model. The horizon line is established where the lines converge. Take the negative of the site or a proof of the negative and trace, with a pen on acetate, an outline of the shape of the projected building—a simplified outline that shows only the shape of the new proposed structure, the eye level (horizon line), and some converging lines to each vanishing point. Cut this down to the size of your camera's ground glass.

This acetate outline must lie flat against the ground glass so that the camera image will not be distorted or obscured. In most reflex cameras the acetate must be put in backwards, as the ground-glass image is reversed by the mirror inside.

With the acetate in the camera, position the camera above the plan or model which has the horizon or eye level drawn on it so that the diminishing lines and horizon lines coincide with the lines on the piece of acetate. Other lines or target points can be included for extra accuracy. Keep moving the camera around the model until a series of pictures has been taken all around the target area. This is to ensure a more accurate selection of views. If the project is a tall office tower, the top will be outside the normal 45-degree cone of vision, which would necessitate tipping the camera to include the top (4). If the camera were moved back far enough to include the top of the building within the 45-degree cone of vision without tipping the camera, it would not be coordinated with the site, unless you had planned a distant view (5).

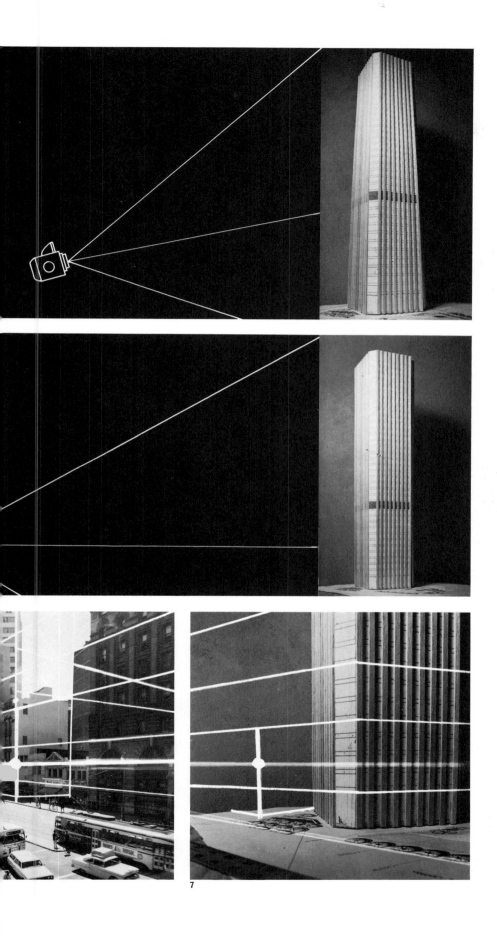

7

Crocker Plaza

Here, the station point was very close to the site, making a wide-angle perspective necessary. However, the model was photographed from the close station point and the resultant photo can be seen to include about a 45-degree angle of view (6,7).

A quick sketch on acetate (8) can determine the results of this exercise. In one instance, it was found that the ground-level view did not show the proposed structure's base or its relationship to the triangular-shaped site. The choice of view was one three stories more or less higher than the street-level view. This showed more activity on the street and a better view of the base of the structure (9).

After determining floor-to-floor heights from the model, these can be translated upward to the full height of the building; then using the vanishing points found from the site photo, the layout can be finished.

8

9

10

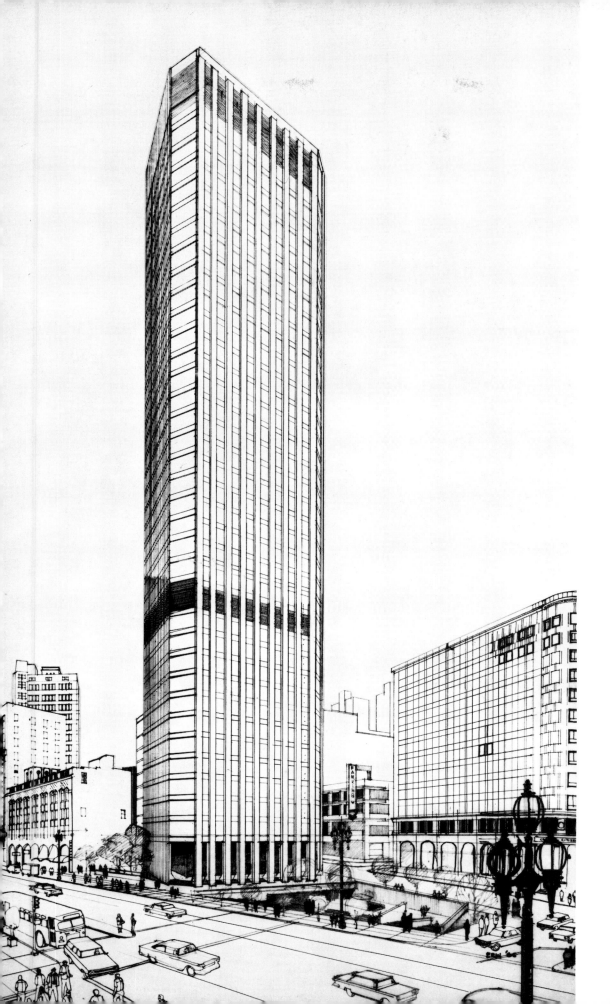

5th and Mission Garage

One of the great perplexities in architectural photography is the control of objects unrelated to the principal subject. Only a small number of these distractions can be removed by the architectural photographer. A delineator, on the other hand, can select what he chooses to include in his rendering. If the appearance of overhead wires is detrimental to the photographer's picture, he must either choose a different viewpoint or remove them from the negative. In a rendering, however, it is an easier process: you simply chose those elements of the site you want to use in the drawing and eliminate the rest. In the rendering shown here the only items that were eliminated were the overhead trolley wires. Whatever you do include, however, should have some purpose to it. This would include items that either determine scale, help provide depth, identify the setting, or lend atmosphere to the drawing. Without one or another of these elements, site coordination would not be necessary.

1

2

3

4

5

Milvia Center

One of the advantages of being able to study site and model together without difficulty or wasted time is that you can quickly see any flaws that might show up in the finished product. This is particularly true when you want to experiment with unusual viewpoints such as these rooftop views. First a number of photos were taken of the site from the most available rooftop, across the street from the proposed building. Of the several studies made, two things were apparent. First, the composition would be unnecessarily dull from that angle. The problem of equal emphasis on the sides of the building was apparent, and it was therefore discarded as a rather poor choice of view. The second view was not much of an improvement since it faced the wrong direction and showed only the intersection of streets and a few adjacent buildings. The rooftop idea was quickly dropped when a study made from the street level was constructed. In each case certain aspects of the site were traced on acetate, placed on the ground glass of the camera, and moved into position to photograph the model from the same station point as the site. The street view not only provided a more interesting composition of the building itself, but gave the opportunity to show some identifying surroundings.

1

2

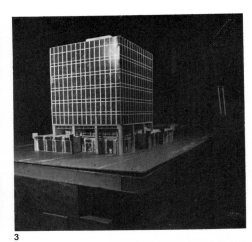

3

4

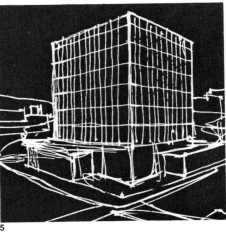

5

6

8

9

Berkeley High School Cafeteria

The decision to do a site-coordinated rendering can come from some seemingly unimportant request, such as to include a recognizable representation of an existing bas-relief sculpture from a nearby existing building. In order to photograph the sculpture, it was necessary to go to the site and take pictures. Several photos were taken of the sculpture on the building during school hours to avoid interference from the students. However, the decision to stay and take additional photographs as the students changed classes provided the real basis for this combination of photograph and drawing. It provided a picture that produced this totally candid scene. The students were unaware that they were to be included in a rendering. In addition you can always find students around who will be more than happy to provide you with any pose you might want.

1

3

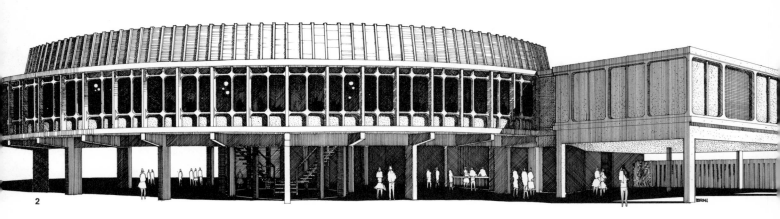

2

Initially the purpose of the photographs was to provide a picture of the relief sculpture; however, upon seeing the results of the excursion in print, it was decided to render the building into the photograph rather than paste pictures on the rendering. And this is exactly what was done. The existing building on the left, the students on the plaza, and the actual plaza itself are photographs. The building was rendered to the proper size separately (3), cut out around its outlines, and set into the photograph. Trees were added as well as foreground planters to soften the harshness of the plaza. Unfortunately the trees were not yet planted when the picture (4) of the actual constructed cafeteria building was taken. In the rendering, one large, unattractive building in the background was eliminated, as it appeared to interfere with the importance of the primary purpose—to illustrate the new cafeteria building and its relationship to an existing structure, a plaza and a bas-relief sculpture.

4

1

2

City College

In order to achieve a convincing site-related drawing, it is not always necessary to stand in one preselected spot and take a picture, thus limiting your view to whatever the camera records. When at the site, take pictures of anything that could possibly be of use, since it costs little or nothing to do compared with the expense of the site trip itself. Once in the studio or office, you might find something that you had not even noticed when at the site and realize that it would make an interesting addition. It is always better to record too much than not enough.

When site pictures for this project were taken, a nearby hill provided a perfect view for the new structure. One further bonus was the fact that the new building would be parallel to the picture that had been taken. This meant that units of measurement could be established along one line. This line was selected to represent the structural system at the front of the building. From that line other portions of the plan were projected in back of this particular measuring line. Since this was in fact a true measuring plane, heights could also be determined.

3

4

5

6

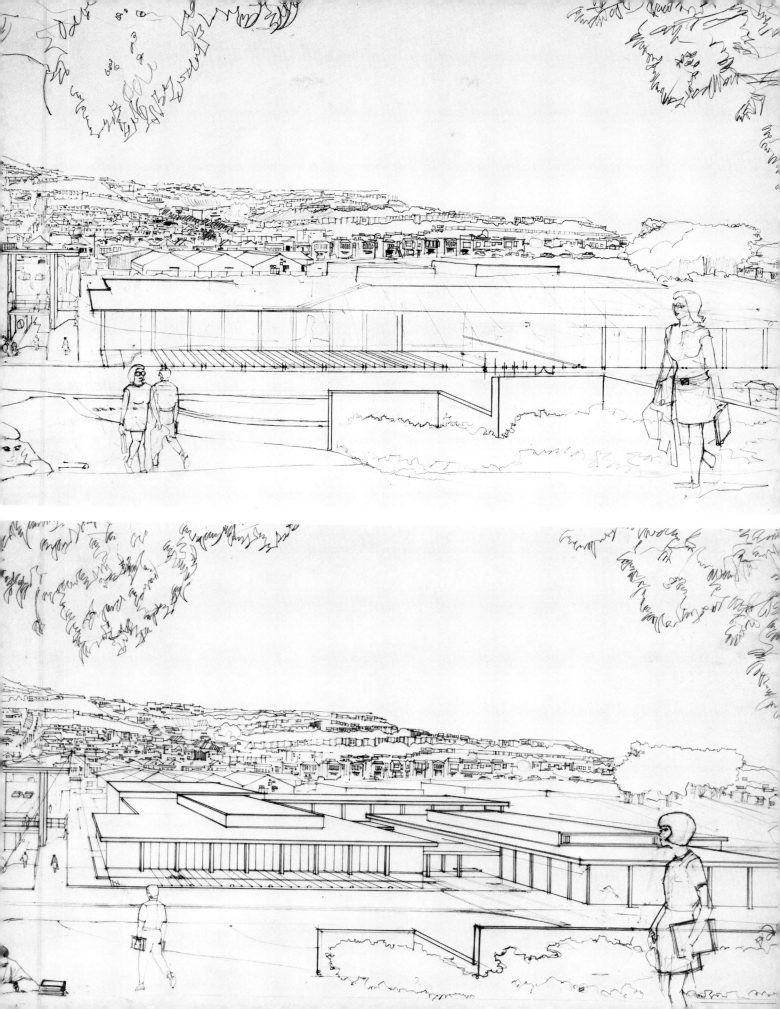

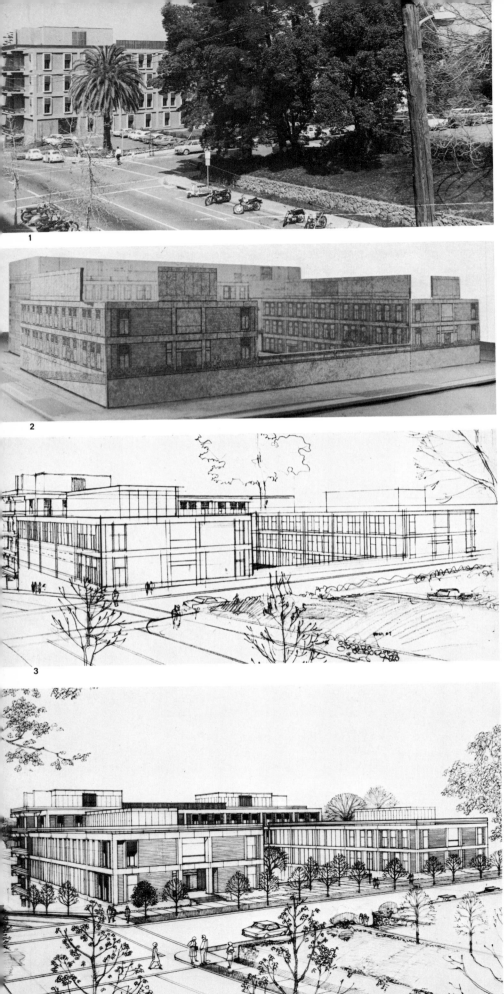

Etcheverry Hall

The requirements for this project, an addition to an existing building, left very little room for maneuvering. The existing building had to be shown in some way, however small. The open courtyard between the two new classroom wings had to be clearly expressed. Finally the eye level should not be higher than the roof of the proposed addition. These requirements fixed a station point and eye level that would have been very easy to satisfy, but for one primary requirement—that it relate to the existing structure.

After the approximate station point was located on the site plan, it was evident that an oblique view across the street would provide just the right view, if the height above the ground could be managed. Fortunately there was another classroom building from which pictures could be taken. Permission was obtained to take the pictures during class break, and a series was taken looking from several different windows toward the site. In the studio the pictures were studied for their relative height and position. Similarly the photos of the model, taken with the aid of an acetate diagram on the ground glass to determine the view, were studied to see how they corresponded to the site photos. Certain target points provided assistance: the horizon line was obtained from the site photo, and the location of the corner of the building determined the inside corner of the existing sidewalk.

From the set of model photos one was found to meet all the requirements of the client. The two negatives were then placed in a projector, enlarged to the size of the finished drawing, and roughly sketched out. After this procedure a more detailed layout was executed in pencil. Many different approaches could have been taken to render this building; however, no other viewpoint would have satisfied the specific requirements imposed. Fortunately, with the aid of the camera these restrictions were not difficult to work with.

4

5

1

Kaiser Hospital

During the design stage of a project several design variations on the same structural scheme may come up for comparison. You could make a separate rendering for each scheme if the building were not too elaborate or the project warranted the extra time and expense. An alternative to this approach can be found in a site-coordinated layout.

The first step is to select a viewpoint favorable to each scheme. Next, select some site photos and project them up to the desired size. The site is drawn up to the point where the actual building will be placed. In this case, the site was quite long, requiring much background work. Then the drawing was sent out and two photographic prints were made from this site drawing. Each layout was then transferred to its respective photograph and the rendering completed as usual.

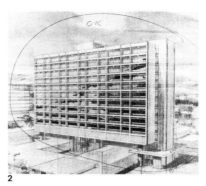

2

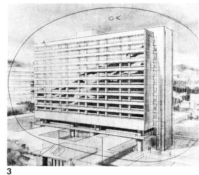

3

4

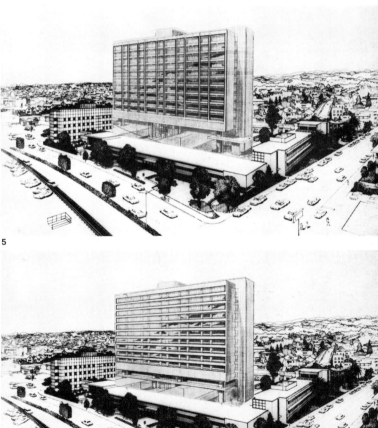

5

6

1

3

4

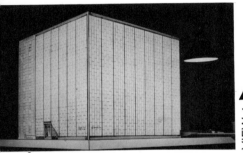

2

VIEW 1 ▲

▼ **VIEW 2**

2

Pacific Tel and Tel

Both additions to existing buildings and future extensions to new buildings call for some form of coordination with an existing situation. Occasionally you might even encounter both in the same project. In addition, you might desire more than one view of this addition to an existing facility and its future extensions.

First the camera is used to record the existing building or at least features of the building that can be useful in setting up the perspective. Next a model is built which indicates the relationship of the new structure to the existing one. The site photo becomes reference for the elements of scale such as figures, cars, and trees, and the model is reference for

the detailed information on the building itself.

Each negative is enlarged to the same scale by using the existing building, which is shown in both the site photo and the model photo, as a measure. These are then traced onto the same piece of paper.

When the initial phase of each view is completed, the drawing is sent out to a photographer and a photographic print of it is made, leaving enough blank white paper to allow space for the rendering of the new addition. This planned future addition is then drawn as a continuation of the photograph, and if this is done in ink, the technique will look identical to that of the initial phase.

1

3

4

5

5

Lincoln Plaza

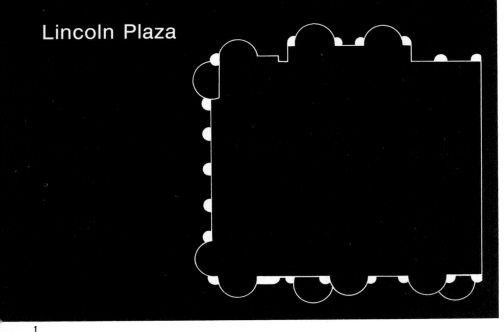

1

Circular forms are always a problem for the perspective artist. Imagine then a series of exposed round structural columns, semiround bay windows intersected by circular balconies, repeated throughout 30 floors. Each circular element for each floor level would be a different ellipse from its immediate neighbor. This would be true for the entire height of the building. It was a wise decision, then, to build a model accurately enough to determine the true positions and relationships of these circular forms.

When the columns were measured in plan, it was discovered that standard half-round wood moldings would be perfect in size. These can be easily purchased at any lumber yard. They were glued onto the elevations, which had been previously taped down to a table. An architectural feature, a concrete band at all floor levels, was provided by using black tape, which is available in many widths. This was wrapped over each of the wooden half-rounds at each floor level. The balconies and bay windows were a little more of a problem due to their large size. However, cardboard tubes provided the answer here. The tubes were cut in half and placed on the elevations. The floor heights, windows, and sills were all drawn flat on a piece of paper then cut out and glued around the tube. Now everything was represented just as it would be in the final structure, except with cardboard and tape. Yet each curve was there, clearly visible.

It would have been a shame to have put all this work into the model without consideration of the environment of the proposed structure. A time was chosen late in the day to photograph the site so that the sun would be very low, which would provide good detail on the existing buildings.

To photograph the model from the same station point required the use of a 4x5 view camera with a rising front. There would be no way to include the top of the building without tilting the camera, thereby distorting somewhat all those hard-earned ellipses.

2

4

3

5

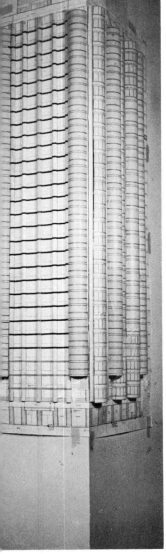

6

1

2

Midtown Office Projects

When you visit a site to take photographs, it is wise to know beforehand if the view is going to be a ground-level or a slightly higher viewpoint. From the ground level cars and trucks can be an interference. Therefore, if you are contemplating such a view, you might even want to try a weekend for the site photos. However, most buildings will be empty on weekends, eliminating any possible higher views.

In the daytime views can be obtained from some buildings, and this will allow you to capture some activity in the street. In any case, the site comes first since it is the most difficult to manage. If site coordination is important, the point from which you take the site photos will more or less dictate the angle from which you will have to shoot the model.

However, if you should find that the model and site do not coincide precisely as planned, all is not lost. Certain perspective controls are available to the professional architectural photographer. These same controls are also available to you even with limited equipment. Perspective distortion can be overcome by simply turning the projector or enlarger from true perpendicular. Thus you can alter the perspective in either direction, horizontal or vertical, until the projected image fits your requirements. Since the building is the main subject, you will want to keep its perspective lines accurate. The site or adjoining buildings on either side can then be adjusted to coincide with the building.

When both the site and building have been projected onto the same working surface, find the vanishing points by tracing to convergence lines from the building. After this is done, all lines on the site or adjacent buildings should be drawn to fit exactly the perspective lines of the project.

4

3

6

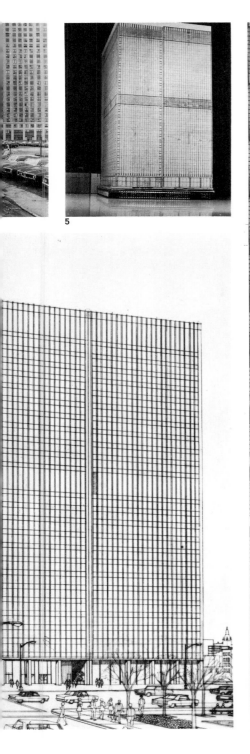

5

7

1

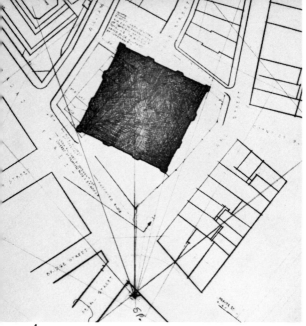

2

Project Downtown

In order to create a truly convincing coordinated layout, you may find certain conditions stretched to the limit. Thus far the sites have been relatively convenient and easy to photograph. From studying the site plan, it was obvious that there was only one spot from which to see the structure pictured here and relate it to the space around it. In addition, the closeness of the station point resulted in a 60-degree wide-angle view of the model alone.

However, since the building completely separated the site left from right, an extreme wide-angle perspective of approximately 100 degrees was attempted. The site on the left was taken on one negative and the site on the right was taken on a second negative. Keeping the lens at the pivot point helps maintain perspective control. Since not all the streets and buildings were at right angles, any minor variations not only would pass unnoticed but would be meaningless.

The limited cone of vision of 60 degrees applies to the building vertically as well. This means that from the desired station point the camera could "see" only to the fourteenth or fifteenth floor. However, with the information obtained from the model photo the actual vanishing points were found. The top of the building was plotted by an extension of the floor-to-floor heights then these were projected to the vanishing point.

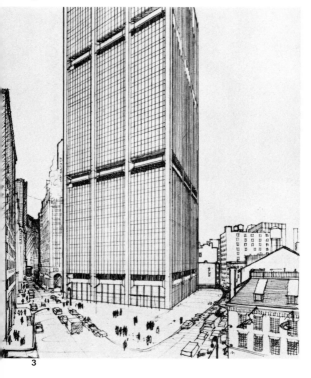

3

4

Chapter 5

Aerial layouts

Urban renewal and the spread of suburban developments have created a growing demand for site-coordinated renderings. More often than not the scope of these projects leaves no choice except to show them from aerial station points. Renderings of projects that cover 2 or 3 acres can easily be created and handled in the studio, using a plan of the project and a camera. But suppose you were asked to render a 900-acre community suburban development, an entire university campus, or an urban redevelopment project that stretched out 10 or 12 miles.

Challenges like these almost always demand good aerial photographs from which to work.

1

2

Aerial Surveys

Once you have decided to accept an assignment for a project requiring a site-coordinated aerial layout, you should check available sources for photographs. You will need to know where they can be obtained, how much they will cost, and how quickly you can get them.

There are three main sources for obtaining aerial photos, one being the commercial aerial photographer, the second a commercial photographer who will take an aerial assignment, and finally, yourself. The services of a commercial aerial photographer will vary from city to city. This man's business is usually to keep an accurate record of the city's development in his area. In most cases he will have taken strictly orthographic views for map-making purposes. His camera is mounted inside the airplane and his equipment is specifically designed for aerial photography. In smaller communities this is the extent of his services, and he would have no other photographic records you could use. He would fly a special assignment for you, but he would most likely wait until he had several assignments to cover in one flight. However, if you have the

3

4

5

time, this is the best possible source, since you would get sharp, accurate pictures that could be used for many purposes. In larger cities, each aerial photographer has a more diverse file. If you buy a picture from his file, you are buying only the print, as he retains the negative and charges you for use only. This is the most economical way to obtain high-quality pictures for your own use.

If you cannot find the exact picture you want from any photographer's file, you can hire a photographer willing to take an aerial assignment. He will use more conventional cameras and film, but his work may not be any less expensive than the aerial photographer. He will expect his usual fee plus the expenses of hiring the plane and pilot. Unless he thoroughly understands what you expect, do not be surprised if his pictures are not taken from the exact angle you had in mind.

If there is no alternative except to take the pictures yourself, some preparation would be in order. You can practice for your aerial venture on the ground. Have someone drive you around town while you take stills from the moving car. Use the car method to get used to switching from camera to camera and to practice loading and unloading film. You will find that once you are airborne, the most simple task seems to take three times as long as it did in the studio.

You might want black and white pictures for enlarging and color pictures for slide projection. In this case a 35mm camera would be wisest for the color and a 2¼ format would be best for the black and white. Do not take a bellows camera, since the wind will tear the bellows right out. Taking two cameras is much easier than changing film in midflight.

For aerial surveys the helicopter has many advantages over the small cabin plane. In either case the door will have to be removed for good clear pictures.

Before departing, make sure you have plenty of film handy and filters on your camera for haze. Even on the clearest day, the haze, not visible from low altitudes, becomes a serious problem. It tends to degrade the photographic quality of the image by reducing its contrast. The effect of the haze differs with the angle of the sun, so if you are taking a series of pictures circumscribing a site, some will show different contrast than others.

While on the ground, familiarize your pilot with your assignment. Use a road map to draw your intended flight pattern around the site. Try to find landmarks such as the two water storage tanks shown in the sequence here. These will guide you and the pilot in finding the site.

Start shooting before you reach the site. This not only provides you with some lead-up material, it also will get you used to the aerial shooting experience. The first noticeable distraction will be the noise of the craft, causing you to wonder if your camera is working. For the first time you will not be able to hear the shutter click as usual. Don't bother to focus, set the camera at infinity, and don't worry about depth of field.

The shutter speeds required are necessarily high, generally 1/250 to 1/500 second will stop the effect of movement. Don't brace yourself against the aircraft, but isolate the camera from any movement.

Finally, remember that no matter what attitude the aircraft is in, the horizon must appear level in the picture or it will look unnatural. In a helicopter this is sometimes a problem, since the craft is not always absolutely level in relation to your site.

The whole ordeal may take only 30 minutes to an hour for most flights within close range of the airport or heliport, and this would not prove too costly. What you will get, usually, is something of value, since you were in control of most of the decision making.

Careful development and storage of this film will be added precaution that your aerial photographic expedition will continue to prove worthwhile in the future.

6

7

Merritt College

In some instances you might feel that an aerial viewpoint is necessary to show the relationships of a complex grouping of structures. At the same time you might not like the detached quality of a truly "bird's eye" viewpoint. It may be possible then, depending upon the site conditions, to arrive at a compromise.

Such was the case of the college campus shown here. The site was located in the foothills, and the campus was to be situated on the top of several hills which would be graded relatively flat. From these hills the vista was unlimited, as can be seen in the site photograph (1) which provided the background for the drawing. The model, built by the architect as a study model, was photographed from a height approximating the peak elevation of a nearby hill. A few photos of indigenous foliage, which were taken while on the site, later proved to be useful. The site photo (1), the model photo (3) and the tree (2) were then all projected onto the same sheet of paper. Each was enlarged to the proper size by moving the projector back and forth until the scale of each coincided. Since the background was simply that, precise coordination was not necessary. The nearby hill was made dominant in the foreground and the scale of trees and textures diminished to give a sense of depth.

1

2

3

4

5

1

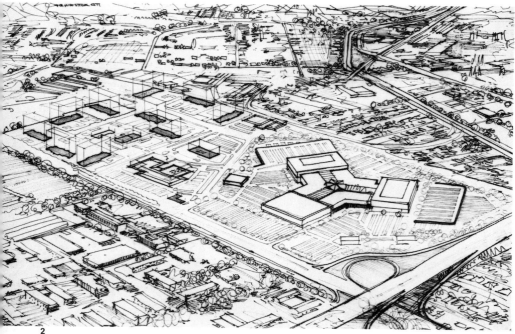

2

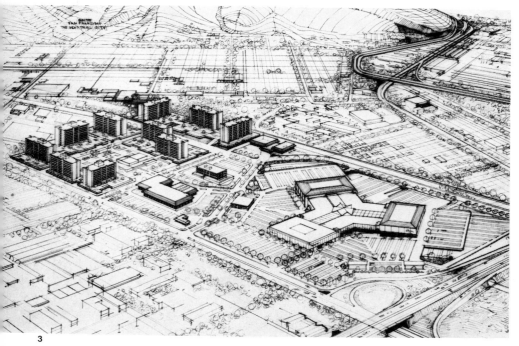

3

Tanforan

An aerial layout can be prepared from a photograph of the site, a photograph of a plan, a photograph of a model, or a combination of all three. The aerial photograph would dictate the angle and height from which you would photograph the plan or model. By looking at the shape of the property on the site photo, you can get an approximate idea of where you must be with the camera in order to duplicate this same viewpoint.

If you take several photographs around this general area, one will probably be close enough to work with. In this instance, exact site coordination is not entirely necessary, so this method of approximating the same relative station point as the aerial photograph is sufficient.

The photograph of the plan is projected up to the size and scale of the aerial photograph. A vertical scale can be determined from the model or by other means described earlier. This vertical scale plus the shape of the apartment tower in plan is all that is necessary to begin the layout. The model, as shown, is more complete, and all that is required is to trace the shape (1,2).

The background and foreground are obtained from the aerial photograph and the vanishing points determined from this photo. Each vanishing point must be located on the horizon line, and due to the irregularly shaped patterns of development around the project, more than 12 vanishing points are required (3).

4

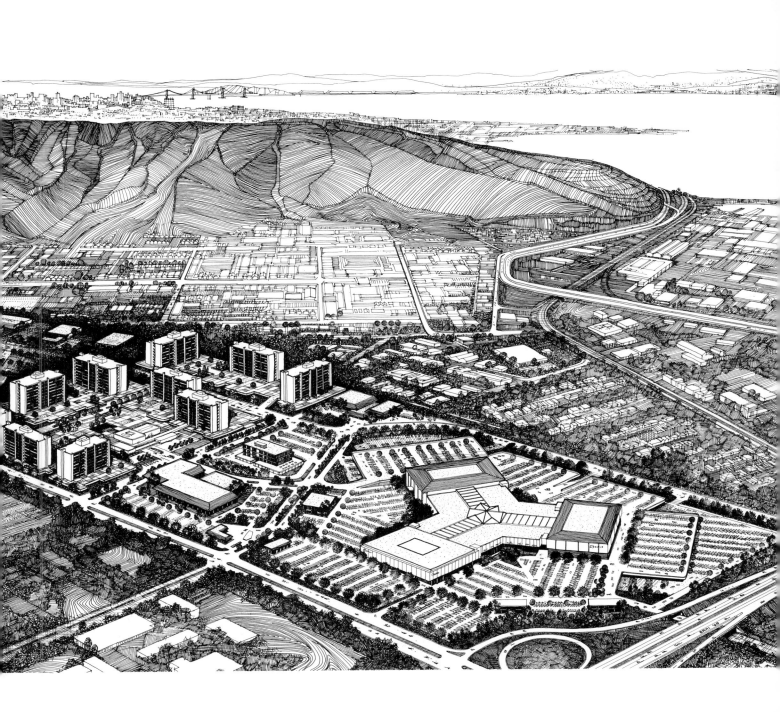

Omnitron

You may discover that a client, such as a board of regents of a university, would like to see your project in a totally realistic setting. This could be accomplished by using a technique called "photodrawing." This is a technique whereby photography is used to establish a scene. Descriptive information is then added to the photograph and the composite picture is then rephotographed. It is an actual representation which is comprehensible by anyone, and its realistic appearance is generally quite convincing.

Everything is dictated by the original photograph, as this will be the basis for the drawing.

In the project shown here, the aerial photograph (1) was taken by a photographer working for the university. The model was also built by the university. The picture of the model (2) was taken by another photographer, and it is not known whether he attempted to coordinate his model photograph with the site. However, upon first examination of the photos, it seemed as if they were taken from the identical location. So each picture was enlarged to the same size and a rough outline was made of each to see how closely they coincided (3). It was decided that they were close enough for the purposes of the rendering. A rough layout of details of the proposed structure was added to this sketchy drawing. Then the final drawing was

1

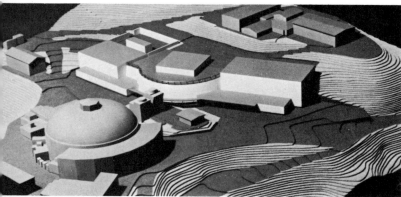

2

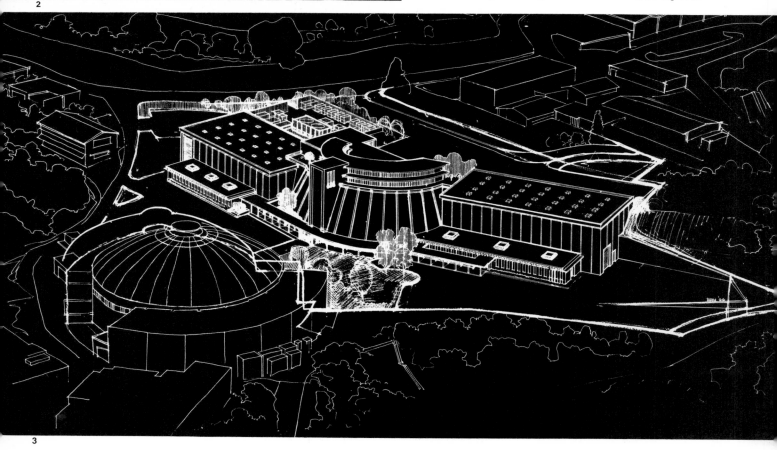

3

prepared on a separate tracing paper overlay, executed in ink line only (4). This tracing was then sent to a photographer who made an enlargement up to the size of the original photograph. The print was made on a heavy-weight mat paper, similar to the thickness of the original site photograph, which (incidentally) was in color. The print of the building was lightly pasted over the site photo with rubber cement and the print cut along outlines that followed natural boundaries such as roads, fences, and building lines. By cutting the two prints at the same time, you will assure a very close fit. The portion of the site photo to be replaced by the rendering was then lifted out and the rendering pasted in its place.

Color and tonal values were then added to the building with ink, pastel, or colored pencil. The colors were matched as closely as possible to the site photo to heighten the effect of realism.

When the drawing was completed in color, there was still a difference in surface texture of the two parts of the drawing. The color photograph of the site, although a mat surface, was glossier than the rendering that was set in. This was overcome by spraying the entire drawing with a mat finish. It could have been sprayed glossy, but the softness of the colors looked better in a mat finish. The entire drawing was later rephotographed on color film and used for reproduction.

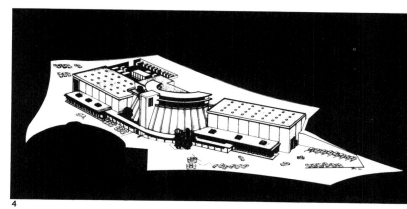

4

5

6

Serramonte

If you were asked to render a 900-acre community subdivision and coordinate it with all existing features of an aerial photograph, you would certainly look to the camera for assistance. Here the photographic system makes short work of an extremely complex layout problem.

To begin, you would make an outline drawing of the shape of the property by tracing it from the aerial photograph at hand. This shape is then cut out of paper and pasted over the property area. Tape this prepared site photograph to a wall and take a picture of it, letting the site area fill up the entire frame. When you get the negative developed, the property will be very clearly outlined.

Next, make a tracing of the property outline on a piece of acetate and trim it down to the size of the negative. Place this acetate in the view finder of the camera. This diagram represents the exact shape of the property recorded on the aerial photographer's camera, from his aerial station point (2).

To find the same station point in relationship to the plane in front of you is relatively simple. With the acetate outline placed on the ground glass, maneuver the camera around until the shapes line up. When all the lines of the acetate diagram line up with those of the plan, take the picture. You have just photographed the plan from the same station point as the aerial photographer who initially took the picture of the site. The rest is easy. Project the negative up until the shape fits the property outline already established, and trace the image onto paper. From here a rough sketch can give an approximation of the shape and size of the new structures. If the site is not flat, assume the plane of the photographed plan to be at some fixed ground elevation and project vertically upward on down from this plane. At this scale, measurements must be in terms of 10 feet or more, since anything less would be inconsequential.

3

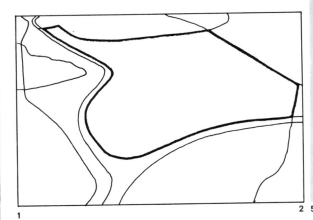

1   2 5

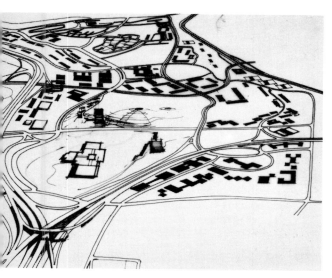
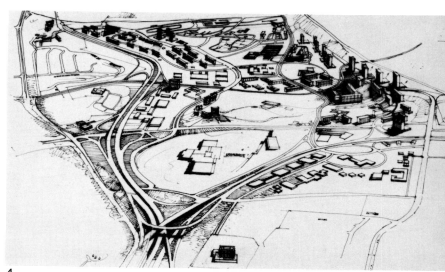

4

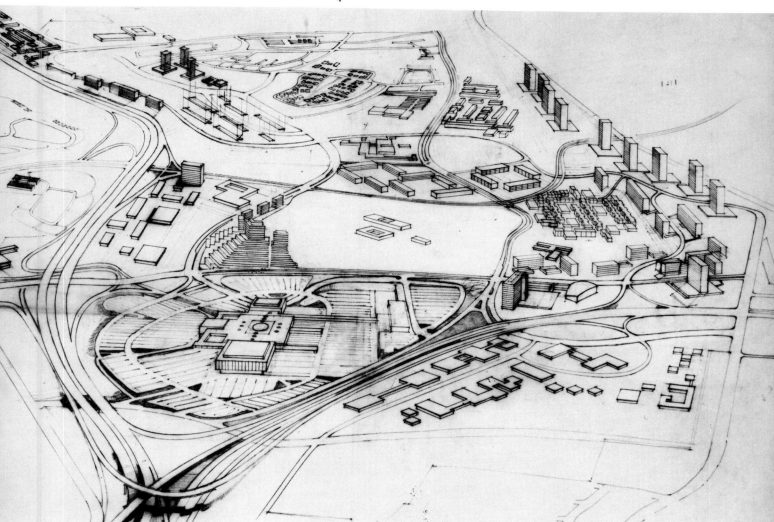

Serramonte

The layout can then be carried out as a separate drawing. When all the basic elements are in, the whole project is rendered with values which emulate the values in the actual aerial photograph. The rendering is then pasted over the photograph and cut out along boundaries that are natural, such as roadways and property outlines. Once set into the aerial photograph, the values can be adjusted to flow naturally from the photo to the drawing. The benefits of this photo-drawing are easy to recognize. Of equal importance, however, is the experience of being able to produce a realistic representation of a project as it would look upon completion.

6

7

8

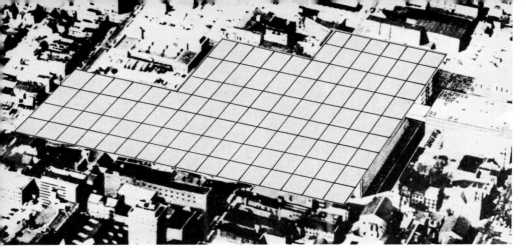

Lancaster Square

Any project in an urban environment that lends itself to a photodrawing technique has many built-in guidelines. Streets are generally at right angles and all vanishing points can be taken directly from the aerial photo. One side will usually have a sharper vanishing point than the other. In the case of the distant vanishing point, you can set up a custom grid to guide you in drawing converging lines. Heights can be taken directly from adjacent buildings.

The rough layout, after all these things are taken into account, is prepared on tracing paper. The final drawing is executed from the layout then photographed and enlarged or reduced to fit into the aerial photo.

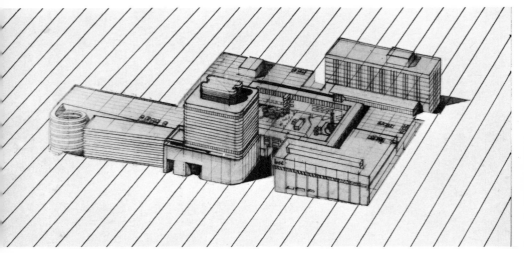

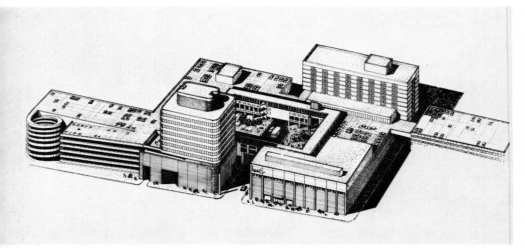

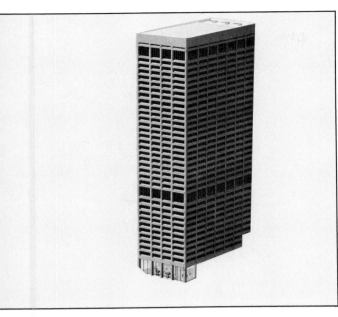

One Beacon Street

Rarely does one get a clear view of a total building even in an aerial. In the case here the site was in a relatively tight, restricted street in Boston. A ground-level viewpoint would have been pointless. In addition, it would not have shown the relationships of the new structure to several architecturally important new projects in that area.

The building was simply rendered separately, in tempera, so that the values of the set-in building matched the values of the black and white photograph. The final composite drawing was completed by placing a photograph of the rendered building directly into the aerial photo and reshooting the composite.

Rendering by: Rudolph Associates
Superimposition by: Jack Horner Pennyroyal

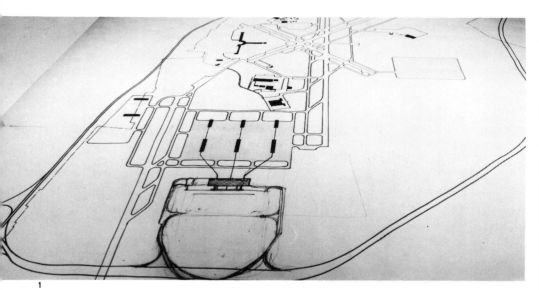

1

2

Greater Pittsburgh Airport

The aerial vantage point could have no more appropriate use than in depicting an airport. If you were attempting to show a single large structure, you might choose an aerial station point. And if you decided to show the entire airport, you would have no other choice. In the example shown here, all that was necessary was to photograph the plan of the runway pattern. The structures were insignificantly small by comparison, and could be laid out from this photograph of the plan.

First a series of photos were taken from many angles and from different heights. The one most appealing put the station point nearly perpendicular to the main pattern of structures and nearly parallel to the main takeoff and landing runways.

This view was enlarged and a pencil layout was executed, roughing in all the structures. Airplanes were included in the layout to dramatize the sense of the aerial approach and to provide scale. This was accomplished by photographing a plastic model airplane. The model plane was attached to a tripod, positioned in space, and photographed in different attitudes in relation to the plan. The one selected for the rendering was meant to give the impression of a plane preparing to land. Without the plane the rendering would have lacked scale. With this problem solved by an inexpensive toy and the camera, the rest of the rendering went smoothly.

3

4

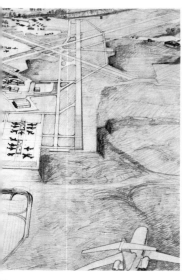
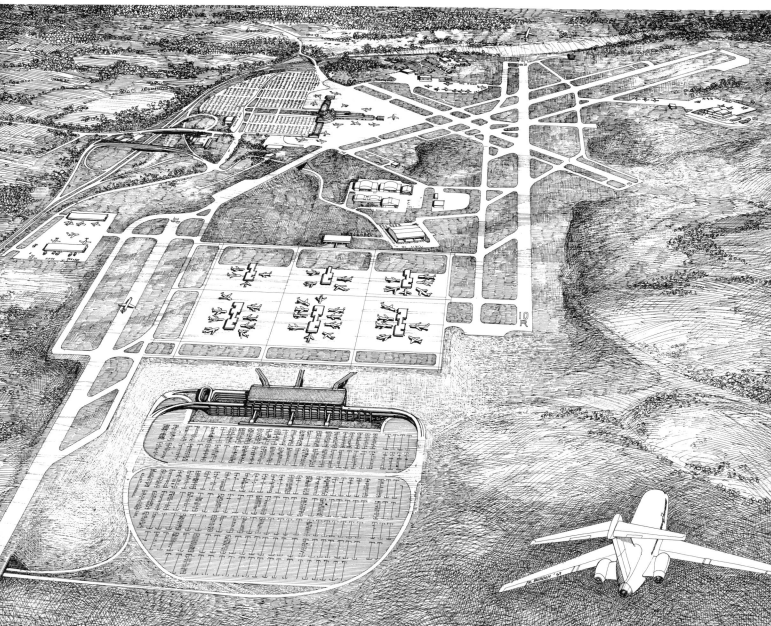

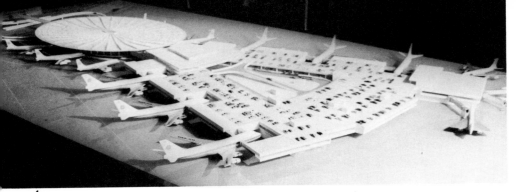

1

2

Pan Am Terminal

The photographic process takes on a new meaning and a new dimension when one is confronted with increasingly more complex problems such as this airport rendering. The problem was to illustrate an addition to an existing facility within the complex of a major international airport. The first clue to a solution was offered by a construction photograph of the existing terminal. Since the composition and angle of view was appropriate to show the new expansion, it was used as a basis from which to photograph the new addition. The camera was positioned high above the model until the image of the model lined up with the acetate outline in the camera viewer. The elliptical terminal building provided an excellent point of reference. Then each of the two pictures, the site photo and the model photo, was enlarged to the same scale. The model picture was cut out and pasted over the site photo in position. This composite picture was then rephotographed and enlarged onto mylar chronaflex instead of paper, yielding a transparent medium on which to work (1,2,3).

The chronoflex photograph was thereafter scratched with an X-acto knife, which yielded a texture in reverse. The purpose was to build up ink textures approaching the values of a photograph and to break down the value quality of the photograph to imitate a drawing. When the two textures merged, the result was a photodrawing, neither photograph nor drawing but containing the best of each. In the final drawing the textures blended together so well that it was difficult to tell where the photograph ended and the drawing began (5).

3

4

5

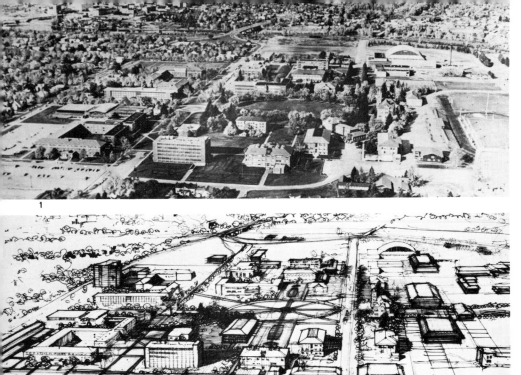

M.S.U.

The relative positioning of buildings such as those on the university campus shown here is most clearly expressed from an aerial viewpoint. In some instances this aerial may be all you would need to produce an accurate layout. New buildings could be positioned by judging their size and shape in relation to the existing buildings.

First a rough sketch is made over the aerial to visualize the position of the new buildings. Then a more careful drawing is executed from this rough layout. As the drawing progresses into the final stage, certain buildings and patterns of landscaping are emphasized and some are diminished in importance. The final resolution of the drawing then becomes one of composition.

1

2

3

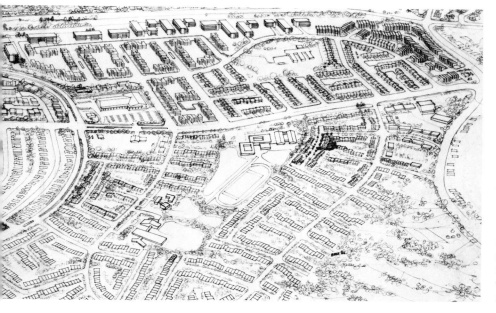

Callan Park

An aerial photograph of a flat piece of property without any distinguishing features is pretty useless as a basis for an aerial rendering.

On the other hand, a land-use plan, which generally contains the size and shape of each structure, would be quite valuable.

A subdivision of several hundred acres could prove to be quite a problem to the delineator who has to locate each house by mechanical means. With a photograph of the land-use plan they are all plotted, accurately, in an instant. In the final ink drawing, emphasis is placed on the higher-density dwellings as a means of composing the picture.

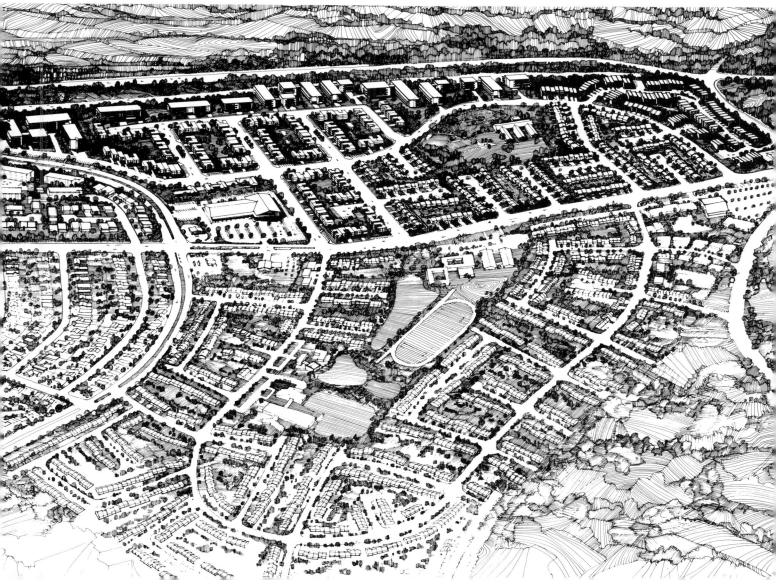

Tudor City

Large-scale buildings require a more encompassing viewpoint, often involving aerial layouts. The scale of these apartment towers would have been difficult to determine if they could not have been shown against some recognizable and accurately scaled buildings. In actuality the buildings would have towered over the United Nations building, which can be seen on the extreme right.

The layout for this drawing was done on tracing paper. This allowed the background buildings to be accurately traced for size and placement. Detail was omitted in all of the background buildings, since it would have proven to be a distracting element. However, each of the new structures was given a richly detailed surface so it would achieve the proper emphasis in the drawing.

East Point

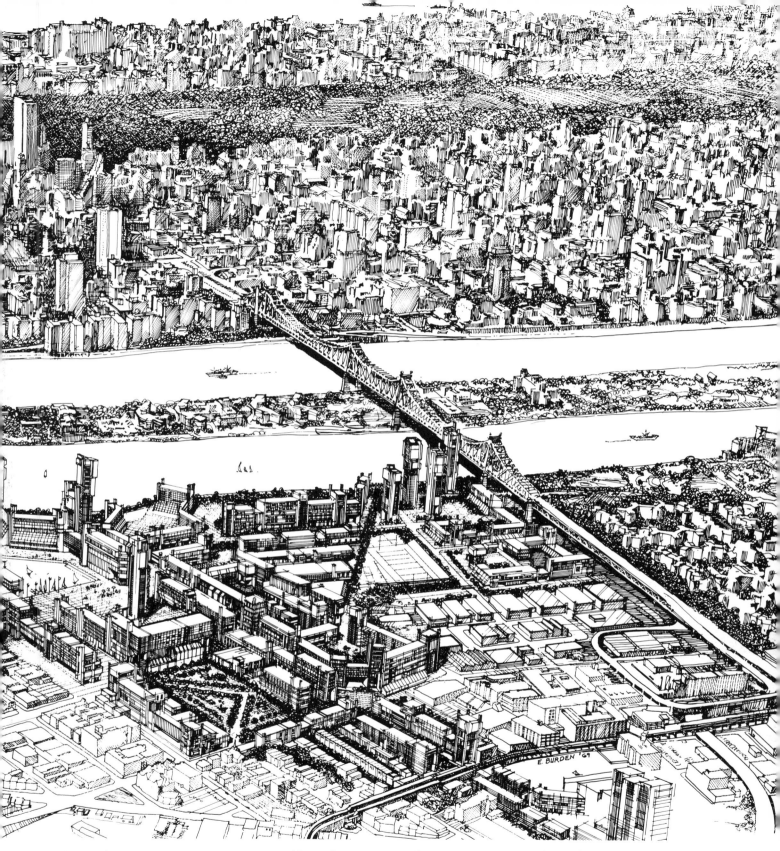

A partial cityscape may present many problems, but foremost of these would be the decisions of how to begin and when to end the drawing.

The basis for any drawing of this scope will most often be an aerial photograph. To determine how to end the drawing, consider the problems involved in the area of your new project and its relationship to the rest of the drawing. Then consider the limit of the drawing, in relationship to these considerations. You will have to begin the drawing from the aerial photograph. Careful examination of the picture will show that it is a three-point perspective.

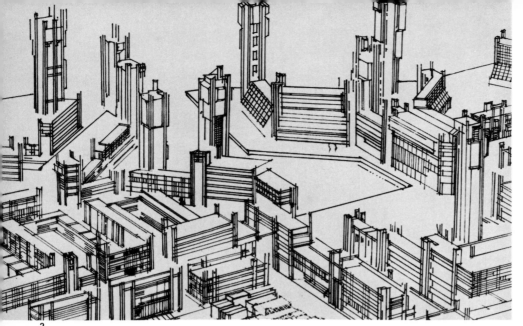

2

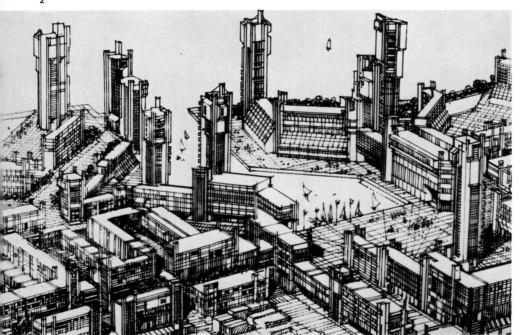

3

East Point

If you draw a line parallel to the images on the extreme left and another line parallel to the images on the extreme right, you will discover that each one will be 5 to 10 degrees off from true vertical, which should appear in the center of the picture.

Using the principle of the custom grid, turned vertically, you can establish the true vanishing point in the third dimension. Unless this is followed, the entire picture will look unnatural. All other vanishing points can be determined directly from the aerial photograph. They will be very far away, resulting in an isometric type of projection. Any sort of grid can be established in plan view, using the existing street patterns to determine where new buildings will go. The entire layout of the plan of the new project should be placed over the aerial first to ensure correct alignment. After this is satisfactory, use the third vanishing point grid to construct the verticals.

Since most redevelopment projects precede actual architectural design by years, you may find some need to let technique become design. Actual floor heights are simply lines, balconies, and projections; window divisions and solids can be created while you draw. Carefully controlled textures can give the impression of architectural elements. For the existing city in the background a looser, sketchy style is used to offer contrast to the crispness of the new development. Here again technique becomes design as dots, strokes, and shading represent an encompassing view of a metropolitan area.

4

5

Cityscapes

Cityscapes, whether partial or more inclusive views, demand rendering layout and technique of an entirely different nature than the single building. It is a layout of many little parts, each one no different from an actual rendering of the same building except for scale. In an aerial rendering of a single building, attention is paid to detail of the building. In the cityscape, the detail is the building. In the layout you must follow all the natural perspective and convergence of the aerial photograph, or it will look peculiar.

Try to look for compositional devices, major arterial highways, lakes, rivers, or bridges. Also try to minimize all detail in the extreme background, foreground, and if possible on each side. This will keep the focus of attention in the center of the drawing. This can be accomplished by keeping edges of the drawing sketchier than the inside portions. However, do not be too concerned with a literal translation of the city itself but look for design elements to add interest to it as a drawing; otherwise the actual aerial photo may be of more use.

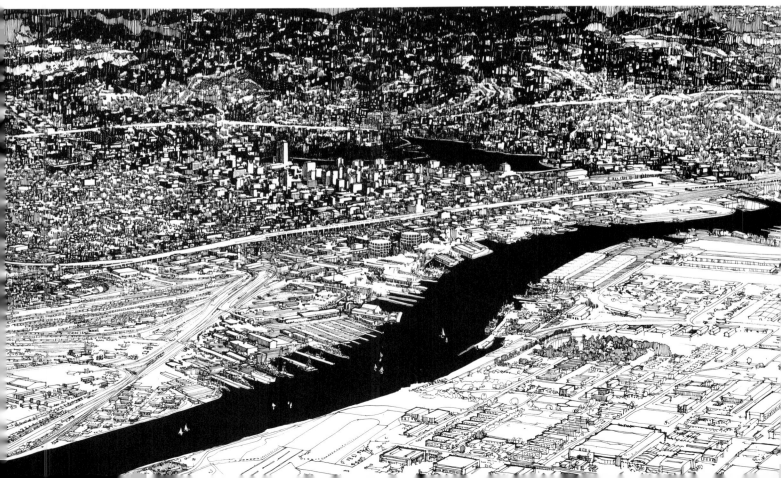

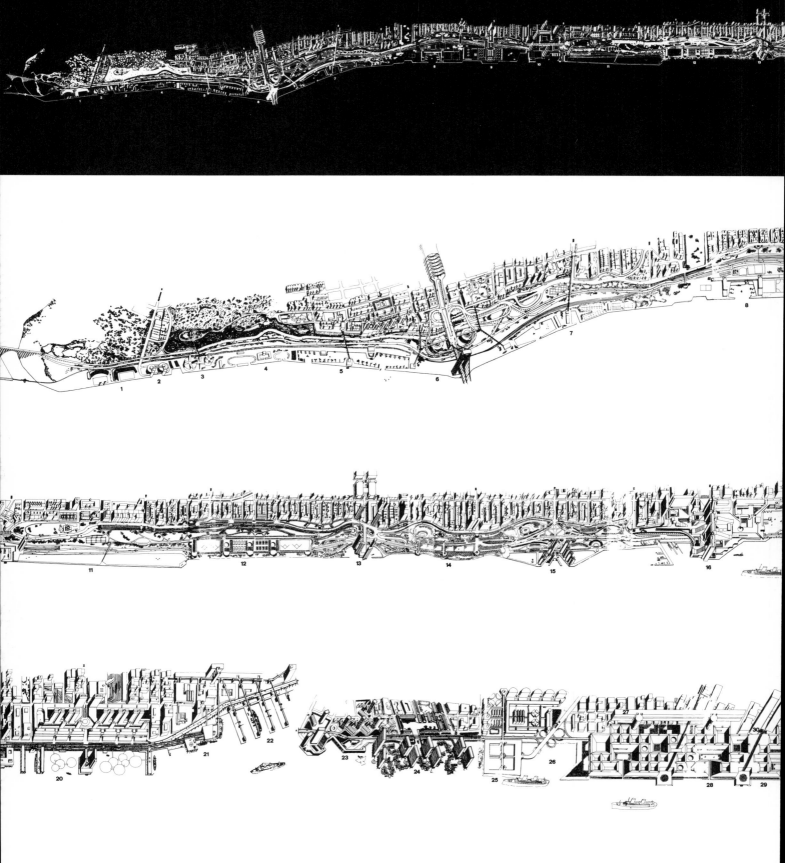

142

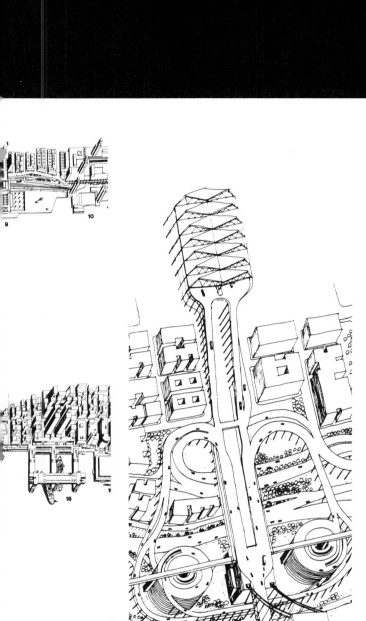

Hudson River Project

Here is the aerial layout carried to its ultimate conclusion: A true isometric drawing based on a pure orthographic plan. This drawing of the entire Hudson Riverfront portion of Manhattan was undertaken by six teams of architects, planners, and architecture students as a total conceptual design of two major arterial traffic ways. One was the Hudson River and its function, and the second the Westside Highway bordering the island of Manhattan. The source for the drawing was the city block maps upon which some new design ideas were incorporated.

The actual drawing was executed by three teams of designers. Therefore, it was imperative to establish certain design and rendering criteria before commencing. Each office worked on its own portion of the drawing. A basic technique was established whereby a standard angle for the isometric projection and a standard vertical scale were settled on.

The actual drawing was over 50 feet long, each section being about 15 feet or more. Since it could never be reproduced at that size, a very loose, almost cartoon style of drawing was agreed upon, to be followed by a joint effort on the actual work.

Even though the drawing was produced by over 50 different people, it has a remarkable coherency. This is the direct result of careful examination of the problems of presenting a project of such enormous scope, then determining the proper solution.

PART THREE
Techniques of drawing

Chapter 6

Entourage: from photographs

Since architecture is created for a certain environment, an architectural rendering is incomplete unless it relates the building to its surroundings. Although the surroundings will differ in every case, certain items will almost always have to be included. These items are figures, trees, and vehicles of all description. To ensure a convincing setting, it becomes of utmost importance to indicate these elements of entourage with some degree of accuracy and skill.

The camera will most likely be used to record the completed building. It can also be used to record isolated objects surrounding the site. These elements, when used properly in a rendering, will lend not only scale to the building, but credibility to the project.

1

2

Trees: In Plan

Trees in plan view are always used when a rendering is done of a site plan. The basic form of a tree in plan is a circle (2), although there are many variations on this pattern.

However, from a height of 200 feet or so, with a Telephoto lens, you can obtain quite a detailed view (3).

There are other methods besides aerial observation which can provide clues for drawing trees in plan view. One such method would be to observe the shadow cast by a tree; at certain times of the day this would be a close resemblance to its projected shape in plan (5). Another method would be to photograph a portion of a tree projecting overhead (6), by pointing the camera straight up at the sky. Take a portion of this picture and repeat it four times (7), making it into a radial design. You can refine this design by making it less symmetrical (8) or by reversing the dark areas (9) for an outline of the

3

4

area (10 and 11). Although this does not give you the actual shape of the tree, it does give you the proper scale and direction of branches and the correct scale of the foliage. The third method is to photograph a tree from the ground at the base of the trunk (12), pointing the camera straight up the trunk. Take four pictures around the trunk. Select a portion of each picture extending outward from the trunk, put the four pieces together (13), and trace over them. A picture of the actual tree from 200 feet (4) and a drawing done in this manner (14) show only minor differences.

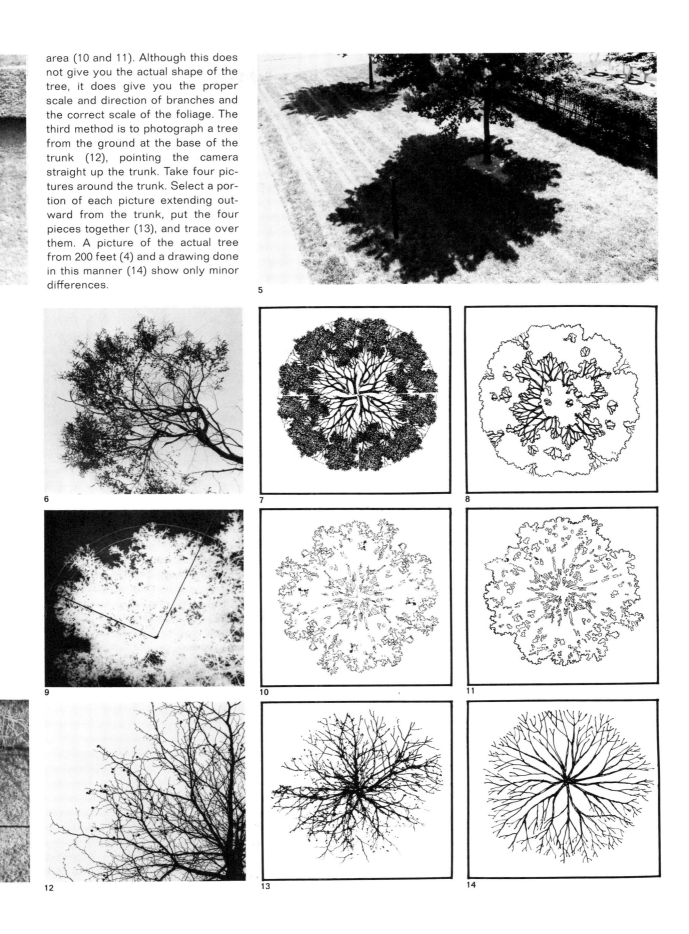

5

6

7

8

9

10

11

12

13

14

1

3

2

5

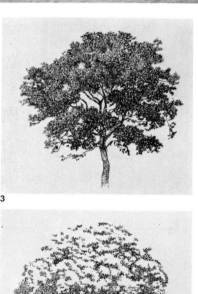

4

7

6

Trees: In Elevation

Trees are most often seen in elevation and are easily photographed this way.

To photograph trees, almost any type of hand-held camera can be used and any ordinary outdoor film will provide satisfactory results. However, certain precautions are necessary. Sunny days are fine for taking pictures provided you can isolate a specimen against a bright object such as a wall (2) or the open sky (4). Otherwise some confusion might result from details of the foliage being lost in the strong shadows. Spring and fall are the best times to photograph most trees, as the heavy summer foliage tends to obscure the structure of the tree completely. The winter outline of a tree (1) is useful for studying the structure but lacks the scale of the foliage. In all cases the bottom of the tree, the underside, will be in shadow, and this may obscure detail of the trunk in some cases. Background trees or buildings (6) will also tend to obscure part of the trunk. However, few trees are so perfectly shaped and balanced that you would want to use them as is (5). Do not hesitate to improve on them when you use them in a drawing.

When trees are used in a rendering, they should first be sketched in roughly (10), in mass outline only. Then the leaves should be added (11), making certain that they are the correct scale for that specimen of tree.

8

9

10

11

12

1

2

3

4

5

Clouds

One of the most common and almost inescapable elements of entourage in an exterior rendering is the inclusion of the sky. Its treatment, then, is sometimes a major consideration, and this will truly vary from rendering to rendering. Some drawings do not require treatment of the sky and then it can be left white. However, some drawings can be improved with a sky tone; it is then a matter of judgment as to the exact treatment it will receive. Sky textures or shaded tones can help to balance a rendering by shifting emphasis. Shaded skys are easily accomplished in nearly every media from pencil to airbrush. Cloud patterns are a different matter. In practically every medium they are difficult and require study for their proper execution.

Photographing skies will give you a record of what most of us take for granted every day. Since cloud patterns constantly change, little attention can be paid to any particular arrangement unless you photograph them. Study of cloud patterns will show that a tremendous variety of form is available.

Good skies are possible with airbrush simply by masking the building and spraying a graded tone in the sky area. In watercolor renderings skies tend to be more dramatic when many different wash techniques are used. In tempera renderings clouds are simply painted over the sky color using opaque paint. In pencil renderings clouds can be easily achieved by various shading methods, including smudging the pencil values to get a softer effect. With powdered pastel, clouds are easiest to achieve—the color is applied by shaving the pastel from the stick form to a powder form and applying it with cotton to the drawing. Clouds can then be suggested by picking up some of the color with a kneaded eraser or tissue. There is quite a bit of flexibility to this method as the clouds can be as soft or as bold and dramatic as you desire with very little effort.

6

7

1

Vehicles

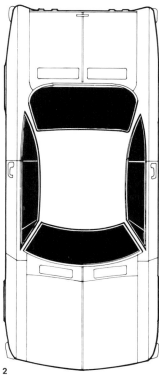

2

Vehicles of all sorts fill our streets (1), highways, and parking lots. It is difficult to imagine any building that does not have some sort of vehicle nearby.

In plan view (2), most cars are generally alike in proportion of the length to the width. However, they differ somewhat in detail. Recording a true plan view of a car can pose a problem, for if you are not directly overhead, you will show more of one side than the other in your picture. When photographing the elevations, however, a distance of 20 to 30 feet is sufficient to overcome perspective, since it is easier to align your camera parallel to the surface that you are shooting.

A rough sketch on acetate would be a good starting point in transferring your photograph to a drawing. Sometimes this sketch is all that is required, but if a carefully drawn elevation is desired, you will have to go over your rough sketch with curves and instruments (4,5).

3

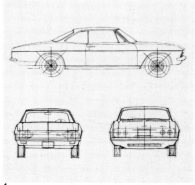

4

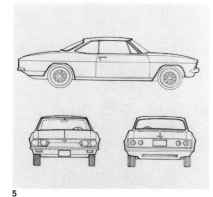

5

6

Obtaining elevation or perspective views of vehicles in the street (6) can be a problem. A parking lot would be the wiser choice, for there you could walk around a stationary vehicle.

Manufacturers of automobiles publish new catalogs each year with many drawings and photographs of their new models. These can be obtained at any showroom or at an auto show, held annually in many areas. Many cars are displayed on continuously revolving platforms which can provide you with an infinite number of pictures.

7

Another source, sometimes overlooked, is the children's toy model car. In the comparison shown here a real car was photographed in a parking lot and the toy car photographed in the studio. The views (8) of the real car were taken from 200 feet above the ground, whereas the model car (9) was conveniently photographed from 2 feet. For all practical purposes the model car will yield equally usable results.

8

9

1

Figures

2

It is true that architectural rendering is not primarily concerned with the representation of the figure, as are other forms of commercial art. However, figures do bring life to a picture, and they give an immediate sense of scale to any drawing.

Photographing people is a relatively easy matter and any hand-held camera will do. It is advisable to use a film with a moderate to fast film speed rating. Your subject is generally not standing still at all times, and you will want to use higher shutter speeds to stop any motion (1).

In plan view the shape of the person can be determined primarily by the shadow. Although figures are not always included in plans, when they are used, the shadow will provide a realistic touch (2,3,4).

Try to photograph people in public places, rather than on sidewalks. The sidewalk is a strong directional element, whereas the openness of a park encourages people to move in different directions, providing a variety of poses (5).

On a Sunday-afternoon stroll you could gather enough views of people for several months of rendering use.

Other sources of figures are newspapers, catalogs, and periodicals. While there are certain fashion illustrators who draw directly from photographs, most do not. The reason is simple: people generally photograph looking heavier than they are. Also, for correctness of posture and stance, the fashion illustrator tries to dramatize the pose. Fashion

4

3

5

156

figures are generally longer, leaner, and most often posed in unrealistic positions (6).

Using photography as a basis for the figure drawing, then, has many merits. If you do not like the pose, you can always alter it to suit your needs. You can also change the appearance of the figure by emphasis on textural changes. You can make the person look younger or older or thinner, or however you might choose. In any event you will be working with a realistic base. How you interpret this into your drawing will be your own choice (7,8).

6

7

8

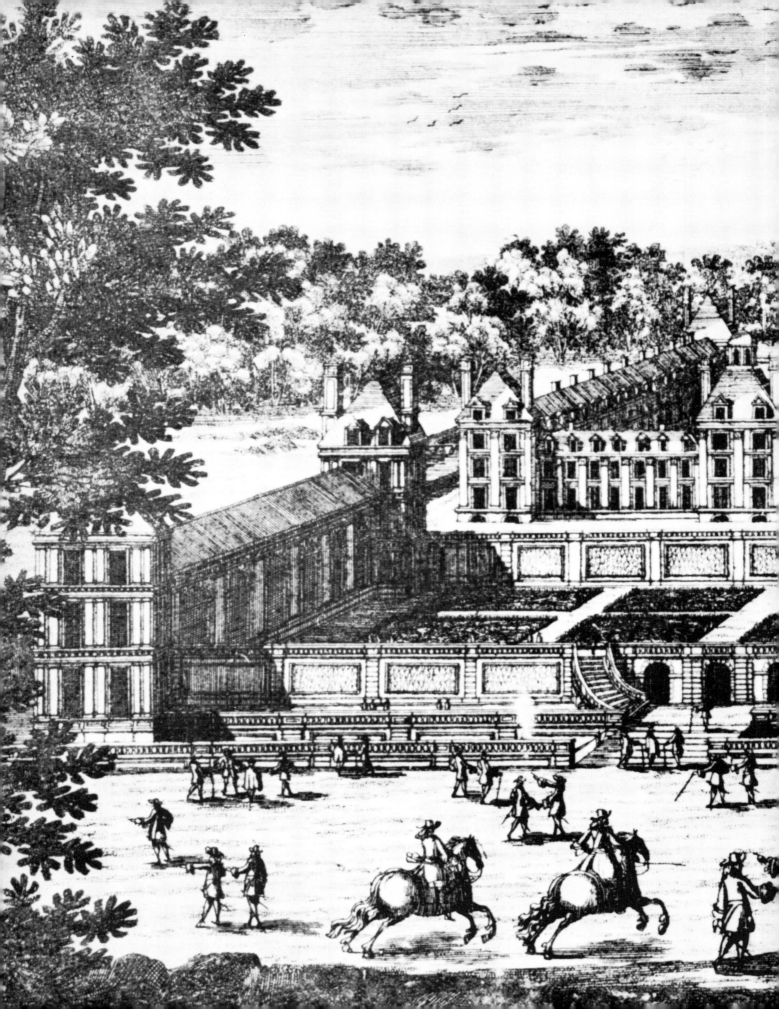

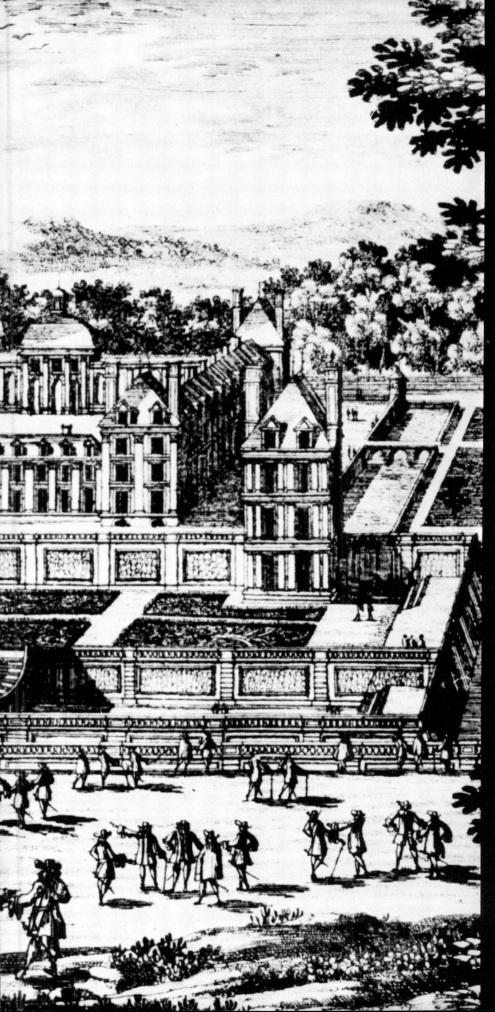

Chapter 7

Entourage: a portfolio of styles

Nature supplies a tremendous amount of material for the delineator to choose from for his guidance and inspiration. He will be required to portray buildings in many different settings. At times these settings, or entourage, will be the main element of the drawing, at other times the entourage will be used only to complement the building.

He should then be familiar with all varieties of trees, bushes, shrubs, and even flowers. He should be familiar with all current makes of cars, and have access to vintage models as well. He should have in his files a collection of pictures which enables him to draw any structure in any circumstance or surrounding

Street Beautification Projects

Some elements of entourage are like objects of architecture at a small scale. They often require the same attention to detail as does a building if they are the main objects in a drawing.

Whenever a vintage car is featured in a drawing, it must be well drawn; otherwise it could destroy the entire drawing. If automobiles are used simply as a backdrop, they should relate to some recognizable model.

To create a successful street scene, many items of entourage are necessary to give the drawing the same sense of vitality that we experience daily, walking down the street.

Drawings by: Mark deNalovy-Rozvadovski

Urban Revitalization

This series of drawings was executed to illustrate a concept of renewal and revitalization of an existing urban area. Here the entire scene is entourage, without the usual focus on one particular building.

The technique of drawing employed here certainly added to this concept of revitalization. The use of rich textures creates a feeling of liveliness. An additional sense of movement and activity comes from the rich display of banners, signs, light standards and planting boxes.

The figures are kept simple in form and do not create any movement of their own. In fact, the manner in which they are treated makes them become stabilizing elements.

Drawings by: Ben Althen

Welfare Island

The overall treatment of this series of drawings is somewhat formal in nature, due to the crisp rendition of the architectural scheme. Certain techniques used to represent the structure were carried over to the representation of the entourage. Flags and banners were treated as elements which echoed the formality of the design.

The main counterbalancing element can be found in the number and placement of figures. Use of the fat figure certainly added a note of informality to the series.

The riverfront aspect of this project was clearly established without placing undue emphasis on water-related activities. The bridge, which occurs in the background of three of the drawings, could have become a distracting element if it had not been carefully rendered with diluted ink to keep the structure subdued.

Drawings by: Ron Love

1

Riverside Projects

In the drawing of the marina (2), buildings are used primarily as a backdrop with the main attention centered on the sailboats, flag, and activity on the pier. A view of the pier shows many items of entourage used to create the marina atmosphere.

In the riverfront drawing (3), structures are again treated as background elements, with the focus placed on the boardwalk activity. Here the elements of entourage are changed slightly to include cyclists and a group of figures flying a kite, as well as the tugboat on the river.

Without this appropriate use of entourage neither drawing would have quite the appeal it now has.

2

3

Drawings by: Mark deNalovy-Rozvadovski

1

Oceanside Projects

One of the most difficult elements in nature to render is water. In the series of drawings shown here by three different delineators, the rendition of the water was an important consideration. The medium employed in all three is the same, namely some form of pencil. In large masses such as are indicated in the oceanside developments shown here, the water was not treated in detail. Rather, it was shown as a large tonal area with a small amount of reflection of objects in and near the water (1,3).

In the drawing of the waterfront apartment complex (2), the water is treated as a dark reflecting surface.

In the oceanfront development the water is also treated as a reflective surface, only the lightness of the sky is given preference, thereby giving a more translucent quality to the water. Highlights were picked up with an eraser to add depth and a sense of calm movement. The reflections of the masts of the boats also heightened the effect of the quiet motion of the water (4).

3

2

4

Drawing by: Brian Burr

Drawing by: Steve Oles

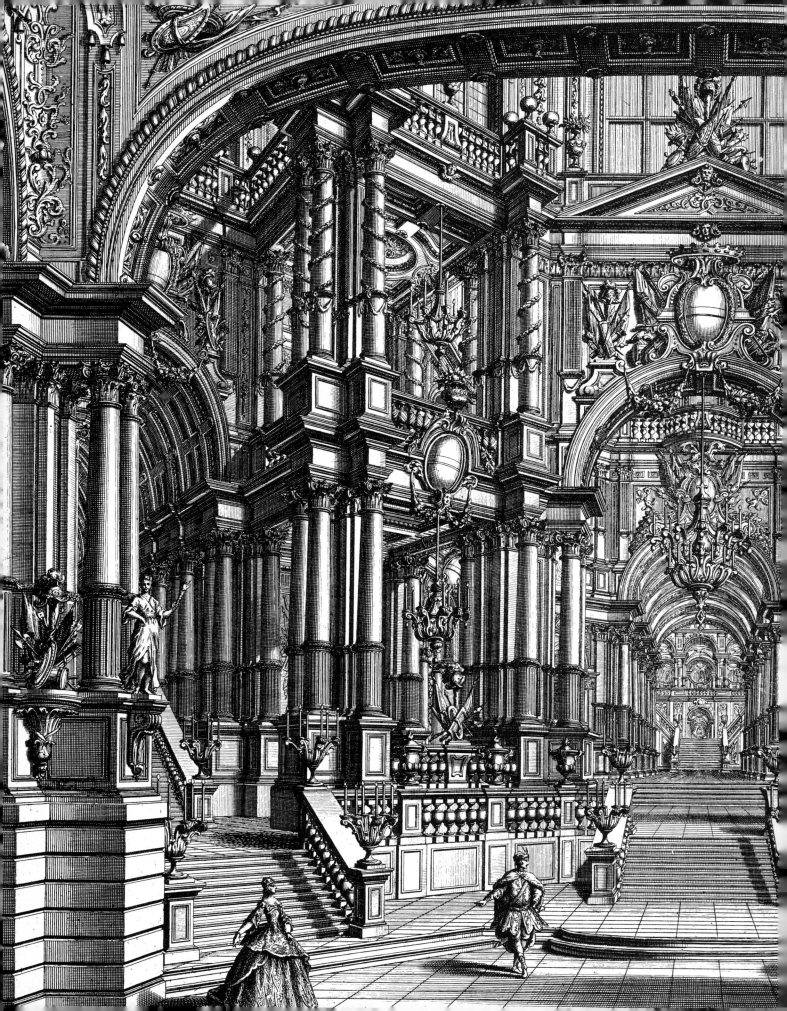

Chapter 8

Entourage: in interiors

Putting figures into an interior perspective is a relatively simple matter. First you have to decide where figures are needed and then determine what their height would be. The easiest method is to place the eye level of an interior at normal eye height.

Larger foreground figures are usually successful at one or both edges of the drawing to establish scale and add depth to the picture. The figures at the extreme edges of the drawing should provide a stopping point for your eye. Therefore, these figures should look back into the drawing. If the foreground figures are left out of interior renderings, they tend to lack the necessary illusion of depth.

Sunvalley Restaurant

Figures can be added to a layout of an interior by first sketching them in roughly on an overlay sheet. By placing this sheet under the layout of the room, you can transfer the figures to the same sheet. This can then be developed into a final drawing.

In the project shown here the figures were drawn in outline only, similar to the rendition of the rest of the room.

Student Union

The rigid formality of this interior space was contrasted sharply by two devices. The technique of drawing did much to soften the lines of the architecture, and the placement of figures added informality to the drawing. The style of dress was kept semicasual, and the simple rendition of the clothes heightened this effect.

The placement and postures of the figures were imaginatively handled. In the lounge area, the atmosphere of relaxed, informal study was successfully portrayed. In the second view, the informal grouping of figures and the simplicity with which they were rendered gives the drawing a relaxed, comfortable feeling. Appropriate use of entourage can be one of the most important considerations in the rendition of architectural interiors.

Drawings by: Gamal ElZoghby

London Hotel

In addition to the task of showing figures for this series of drawing interiors there was the problem of showing furniture, tables and chairs, plants, and interior wall treatment.

In the coffee shop figures had to be shown seated in booths, at tables, and at the counter.

In the view of the cocktail lounge, the figures are very carefully placed in groups. Since the figures are rendered lightly, almost transparent, they do not dominate the drawing yet contribute greatly to its success.

Drawings by: Mark deNalovy-Rozvadovski

Luchow's

The free-flowing forms of art nouveau design gave this interior room an informal appearance. By contrast, the figures were treated very formally, both in their manner of dress and the technique employed in drawing them. Each of the three drawings is a very carefully controlled composition of art nouveau decor and contemporary figures. To further emphasize the completely stylistic quality of these drawings, they were placed within a frame reminiscent of many illustrations from the art nouveau era.

Kent Memorial Library

To capture the quality of the relaxed environment necessary for reading books, a soft pencil technique was used for this interior. The entire room was entourage with walls of books substituting for a hard architectural treatment.

Each reading area had a windowed view of the garden court through which light would filter in. The extremely delicate shading and absence of ruled lines adds to the softness of the effect. Sunlight was further emphasized by rendering the tree in the courtyard in strong highlight tones, again avoiding linear definition or harsh shadows.

Drawing by: J. Henderson Barr

Hinge Block

The placement of figures and trees in this interior rendering is secondary to a device sometimes overlooked in interior views. The wide range of tonal values employed here is the feature which gives this drawing its most characteristic quality. The values of light and shade have been very carefully studied and quite consciously controlled.

In addition to the rendition of light and shade, other qualities of light are given expression here. These include reflected light from floor surfaces and filtered and diffused light from the transparent roof enclosure.

The ideal medium to express these nuances of value is the pencil. A shading range from broad dark to delicate off-white is possible with pencil. It is an extremely versatile medium useful in creating the many moods demanded in interior renderings.

Drawing by: Steve Oles

Light in Interiors

Practically any subject can be rendered in pencil. However, being a pointed medium, it is well suited to render the detail usually associated with interiors (1,2).

In addition it can produce patterns which simulate varying tones of light and shade by overlapping textures.

In the two renderings of a subway station the effect of sunlight was created mostly by the strong shadows cast on light surfaces from the ceiling grid overhead. In addition, strong shadow patterns were projected onto the floor, thereby increasing the definition of the floor.

One of the most dramatic effects of light in this interior rendering was created by employing a device seldom found in interiors (3).

This device was the use of a third vanishing point in the vertical plane, which dramatized the effect of light streaming in from an overhead source.

The drawing was meticulously constructed so that each floor level diminished from the preceding one.

Following this, the drawing was executed in ink and airbrush. When the entire rendering was completed, the soft shafts of light were sprayed on the drawing.

Drawings by:
Arnold Prato

1

2

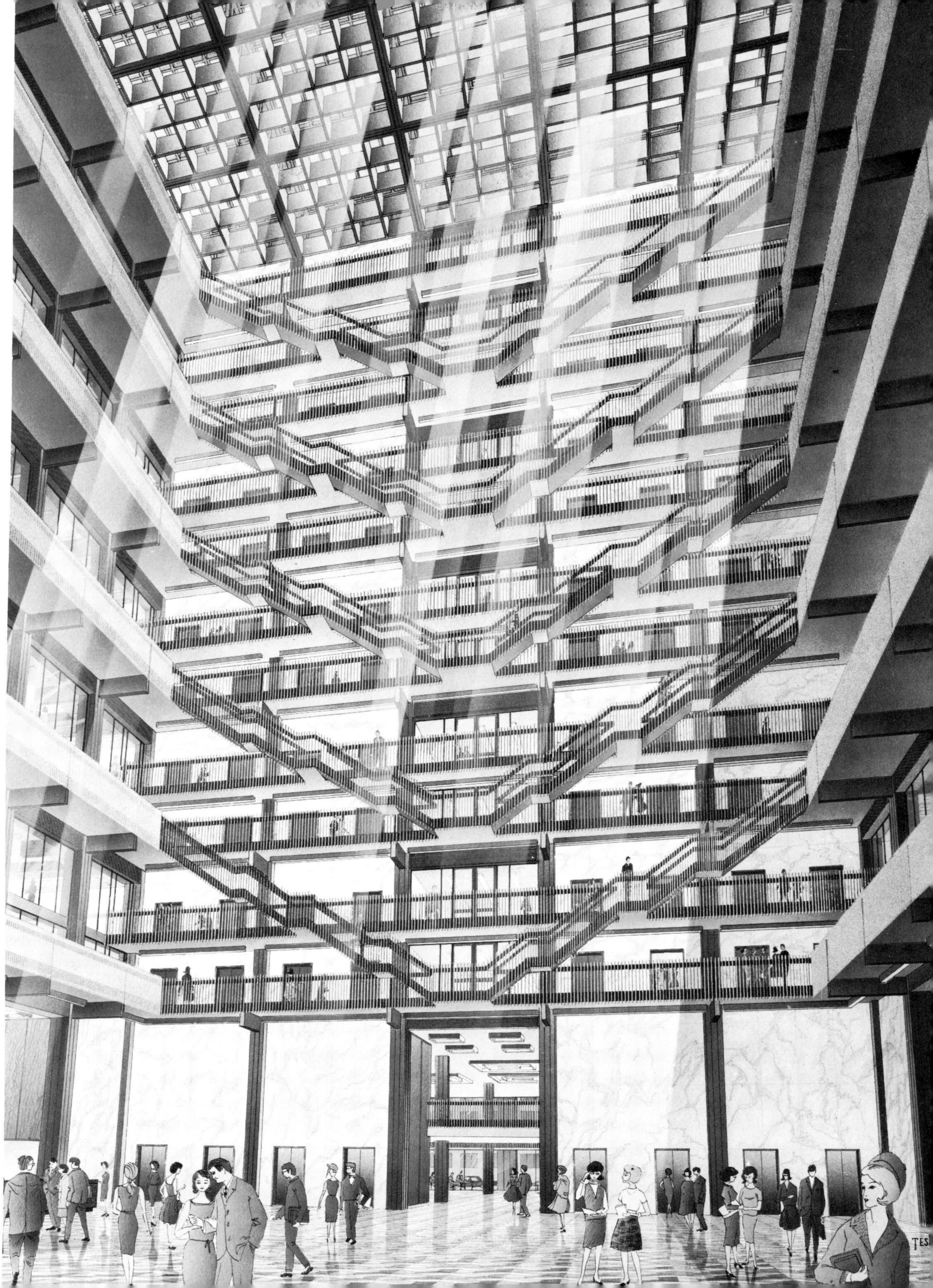

3 Drawing by: Tesla

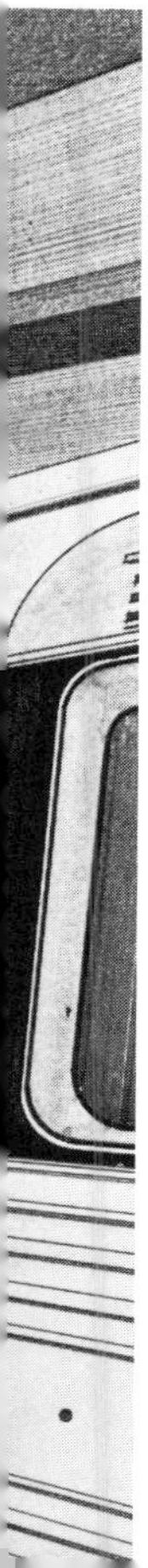

Chapter 9

Drawing techniques

The most exciting part of any rendering is the actual act of drawing. This
is where the rendering gets its main
characteristics. This is where the
individual artist expresses his own
hand.

In commercial artwork, the artist
creates a total picture, whether it is
based on reality or not, so his style
and subject matter are inseparable.
A delineator is necessarily limited to
showing a real building in a realistic
setting. How well he manages to do
this is a mark of his ability. In order
to give the mechanical layout he
produced some life, he must rely on
his technique to create a sense of
the real from dots and dashes,
strokes and textures.

Lawrence Perron

Here the pencil takes on a new dimension. If used by itself, it will produce effects of light and shade by varying the intensities or directions of the stroke of the pencil.

If the same drawing were done on a board that had previously been prepared with gesso, the result would be a combination of the pencil strokes and the prearranged texture of the gesso. This combination, when used successfully, gives a spontaneous quality to the drawing.

In the past, the pencil delineator could rely on the detailing of the building for interest in his drawing. Today, however, new techniques must be evolved to appropriately depict the architectural forms of today.

190

Steve Oles

In choosing a medium to accommodate and convey his own concept of
reality in an architectural rendering,
Steve Oles was attracted to the use
of pencil. The pencil allows a maximum range of expression through
tonal values. Ease of control, pre-
dictability, and variability of texture
were equally important considerations.

The pencil used to produce the
drawing shown here was of the wax-
base type rather than the graphite
or carbon pencil. These latter two
tend to smudge easily, and the
graphite will produce a reflective
surface when heavily applied. It is
also difficult to get an intense black
with a graphite pencil.

These are all important considerations in attempting to produce
renderings which have a quality of
freshness and high degree of con-
sistency.

Gamal ElZoghby

In this aerial view of a city square the board was not prepared with gesso. The buildings were all outlined freehand in ink and then some general tones were applied with charcoal. Finally shades and shadows and fine detail were put in with pencil.

The combination of media, whether it be ink, gesso, pencil, or charcoal, can result in an extremely wide range of expression.

J. Henderson Barr

This drawing displays an extreme amount of control and careful balancing of tonal qualities. Shadow areas are not too dark, and the general quality of filtered and reflected light is very skillfully handled. All tones are built up from overlapping textures which are all very carefully studied and controlled. The interior courtyard is handled very effectively by showing a central ornamental tree in light tones against a darker interior. The total cohesiveness of this drawing was achieved by the careful relationships of the textures.

J. Henderson Barr

This drawing was executed on transparent mylar, drawn directly over a very carefully detailed line drawing underlay. All the final drawing was done freehand, to avoid harsh sharp lines. The technique used was short, small strokes using a black wax-based pencil. Using this technique, the lightest tones in the drawing are put in first, and then these are gradually built up to the darkest values.

Arnold Prato

This drawing indicates the linear style of drawing that Arnold Prato has developed. The technique here is based more on considerations of the proper rendition of form than on any particular medium used. Values can be applied either by ink outlines, by gradation of pencil tones, or by applying an ink wash over a line drawing. In each case it is the design that controls the choice of technique, and this must be reevaluated each time.

Davis Bité

Inspiration for some of the elaborate textures that Davis developed in the evolution of his style can be traced to his admiration of engravings of the old masters. These include such masters as Gustave Doré, Piranesi, and Bibienna. He then developed the style of using a carefully controlled overlapping of lines to produce the values he wants.

However, even the most carefully studied area still has an element of freshness to it which comes from his very bold use of the ink line.

Considerations of light and shade and of reflected light were all carefully balanced, yet the total effect of this technique is still one of spontaneity.

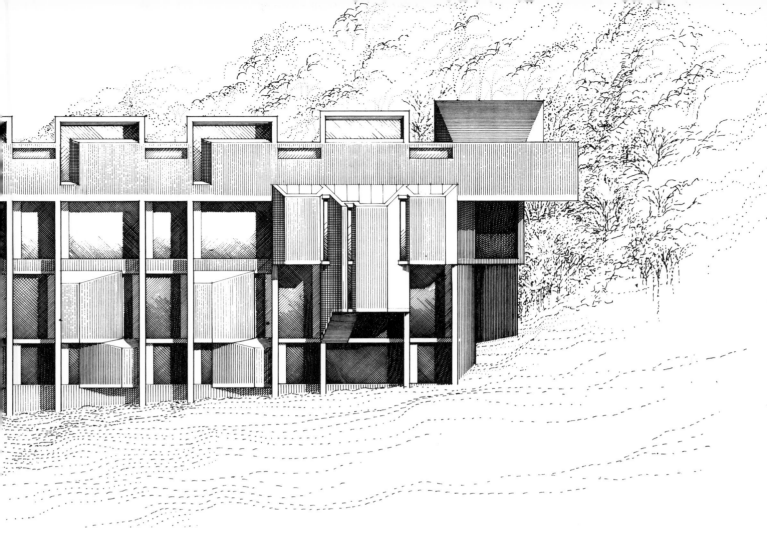

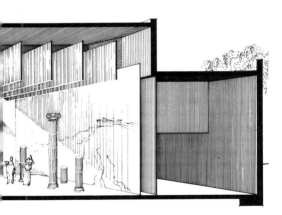

Here a rendering technique is used to render an elevation and section. Usually drawings of this nature are done extremely large and the values studied in the reducing glass to be sure that they hold up at a reduced scale. The rich textures created in the interior cutaway section are produced by many layers of overlapping cross-hatching. First established by a vertical line, then by 45-degree strokes as the second direction, and then an opposite 45-degree stroke if the area still needs to be darker. And lastly, lines emanating from a station point will add additional hatching if necessary. In addition to this, the closeness of the lines can control to a great degree the value on any given area.

Davis Bité

Davis Bité

Here ink-line work is effectively combined with free-hand ink textures. The clear-cut angularity of the structures is further emphasized and enhanced by the textural treatment in the foreground and sky. The use of hatching to build up the darker values was very skillfully handled here. Certainly the architectural forms were given a new dimension by the creative use of lines.

Albert Lorenz

Line work can be carried to almost any degree of intensity, even to an almost solid black. This technique combined with a loose freehand texture can also be very effective.

Here the building was very heavily rendered with ink lines and overlapping crosshatching. Then to increase the contrast between building and sky a free hand texture was used behind the structure. This dark sky heightens the effect of light on the richly detailed plaza and streets below.

Ron Love

The technique used in this drawing intended to show the structures by means of tonal contrast rather than by means of outline. This was achieved by the use of value changes made up primarily of cross-hatching and stippling. To control these tonal changes, they were all worked out beforehand in pencil and then drawn in ink.

This drawing was executed primarily for reproduction purposes. This crisp linear style would yield excellent line engravings for magazine reproduction.

In order to maintain the same open quality throughout the entire drawing, the foliage was treated very loosely. This technique allowed the page to become an integral part of the drawing.

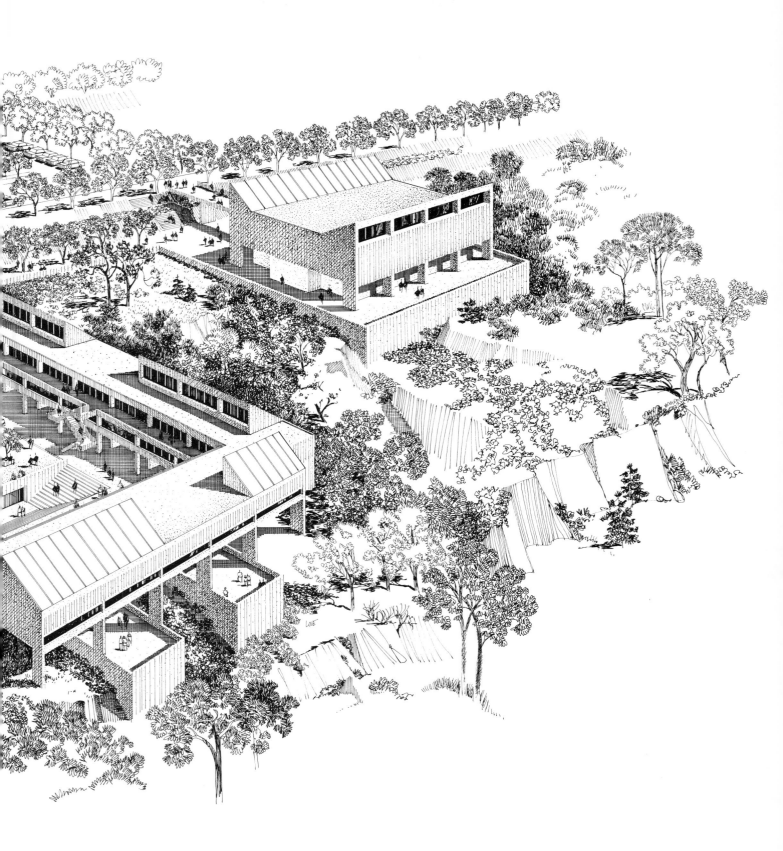

Brian Burr All the values in this drawing were created with lines. After the basic drawing was laid out in pencil on an illustration board, the main elements were inked in. The single use of parallel lines to create a simple texture was followed by a series of cross-hatching to build up the darker areas.

The trees were rendered as winter outline to avoid obscuring the detail on the plaza. Water in the pool in the center of the plaza was made reflective by the use of multiple cross-hatchings.

Brian Burr

Another method of building up the tonal values of a drawing can be seen here. The ink-line work and textures for the entire drawing were carried to completion first. Trees were completely rendered and the grass textures put in. Materials were all carefully rendered on the structures and all the values put in with line work.

Then the drawing was masked area by area and additional values were put in by spraying the unmasked area with ink in an airbrush. The tones applied were kept necessarily light because the values had already been carried so far in the ink drawing underneath. After each of the several areas had been sprayed, the sky tone was put in.

Mark deNalovy-Rozvadovski

Following a pencil layout done on the board, Mark begins to draw in the entourage in ink. This gives a freshness and spontaneity to the figures and keeps them light and airy. It also strengthens the suggestion of movement. After the entourage is drawn in ink, work is begun on the structure. As soon as the entire building is outlined, all the pencil is removed, and from that point on the drawing becomes art. From then on, the entire drawing is worked up to completion all at once. This allows it to be treated as a total composition. In each case the building is rendered as a solid object, and the rest of the drawing supports the composition. By treating the ground plane and the figures lightly, the effect of movement is maintained.

Ron Love

This type of rendering is approached as a regular watercolor rendering rather than as an ink drawing with a wash of color over it. The entire value pattern and color are worked out in advance, much the same as in a tempera rendering. The line drawing is done on watercolor board using waterproof ink. The color is then applied using various methods of masking, much like an airbrush drawing.

Gamal ElZoghby

In this drawing, the entire form was built up from specially created textural patterns. All outlines were created by placing different textures next to each other. All other lines were formed by dots and dashes.

After the drawing was completely worked out with these textures, certain portions were masked and sprayed with airbrush. These gave the opportunity to create new values by spraying some of the textures with a darker value than others.

Tesla

One of the most sophisticated techniques of all is the use of ink and airbrush.

Tesla has received many awards for his drawings, executed in black and white and in color. Most noticeable in his renderings are the subtle and sophisticated rendition of forms and the dramatic use of light.

In an airbrush drawing the ink-line work supplies the outline and architectural details of the building. After the drawing is completed in ink, the airbrush is used to supply tones and values to the sky and various parts of the building.

Tesla uses the three-point perspective whenever an aerial viewpoint is used and whenever the building exceeds a certain height above the observer. This dramatic use of perspective plus the skillful handling of light and shade is what separates these from the ordinary colored rendering.

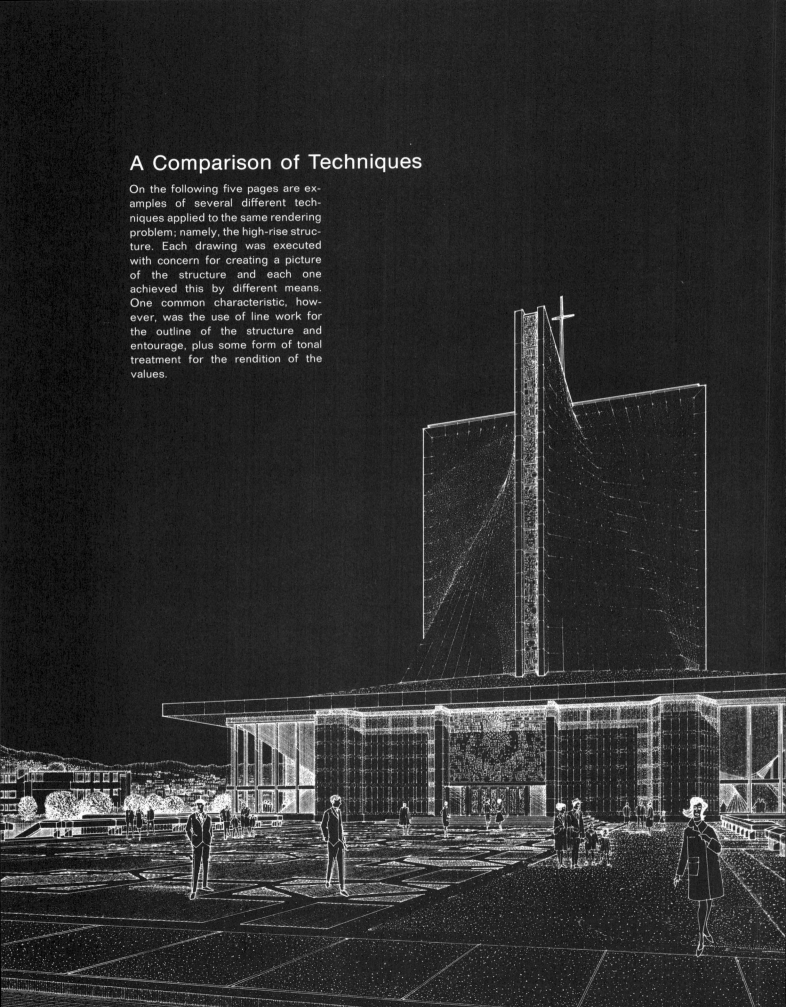

A Comparison of Techniques

On the following five pages are examples of several different techniques applied to the same rendering problem; namely, the high-rise structure. Each drawing was executed with concern for creating a picture of the structure and each one achieved this by different means. One common characteristic, however, was the use of line work for the outline of the structure and entourage, plus some form of tonal treatment for the rendition of the values.

Project Downtown Ernest Burden Ink line and airbrush

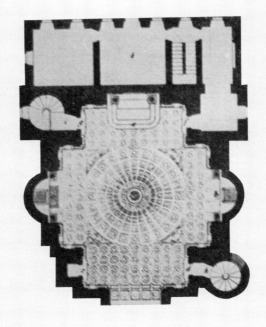

Chapter 10

Coordinated series

Architectural renderings are usually supplementary material to the architect's own plans, sections, and elevations. Very often a single rendering of a large complex is inadequate to explain the scope of the project. In this case, a series of coordinated drawings would be more advantageous.

Certain basic principles should be recalled from previous chapters in relation to any series, namely, camera movement, composition, and camera angle.

What I have chosen to show in this chapter are projects where some thought and purpose is given to the sequence of views and to the coordination of techniques in each case.

175 Park Avenue

This entire series was rendered in pencil on prepared gesso board.

The three views were selected by the architect to relate the new tower to the existing terminal at Grand Central Station. An environmental sketch of the base illustrated a pedestrian's view of the concourse level. The aerial view clearly related the scale of the new building to many existing landmarks, such as Rockefeller Center, left, and the Chrysler Building, on the extreme right.

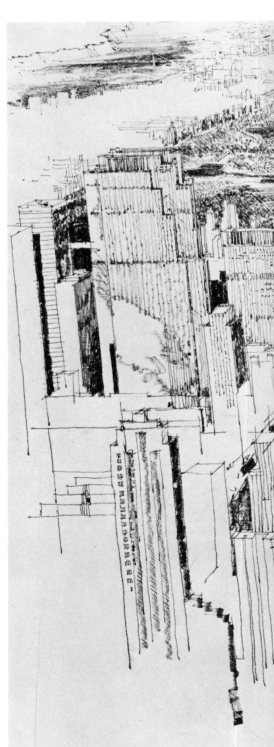

Drawings by: Lawrence Perron

L PERRON

Wilson Commons

Several trials were made to correlate these two interior views of the same space, each one taken 180 degrees from the other. The first attempt was to use the same station point for both views. This did not adequately show the space in one of the two views. Next, views using the same elevation but different station points for each were tried. Finally selected were two views

taken from bridges on which an observer would actually stand. Therefore, in each view one can see a scale figure, represented as a photographer, at the location of the station point for the other view. Each view was then portrayed as occurring at the same time of day, showing consistent sun angles. Each drawing was executed in pencil.

Drawings by: Steve Oles

Mercy Hospital

A very crisp linear pencil technique executed on tracing paper served as the medium for all four views. This technique gives the appearance of ink in the clarity of the line yet has an overall softer tonal value.

This series of renderings shows the completion of a multiphased expansion program. This program was designed to replace eventually all existing facilities of the nearly century-old hospital.

The first phase of construction, the tower building, rendered in each view in outline only, serves to provide the unifying element for each view.

Drawings by: Arnold Prato

Forrestal Building

Due to zoning height restrictions all federal office buildings in Washington, D.C., are of necessity long and low. In order to show a building of this size, several views were necessary.

In addition to the crisp linear ink technique which binds the series together, some common traits can be found in the selection of viewpoints. The majority of the drawings are one-point, or parallel, perspectives which lend a certain amount of stability to the series. The rendered sectional perspective helps to explain the space depicted in at least two of the renderings and therefore becomes an important part of the series.

Focus was controlled by eliminating detail at the edges of the drawing and by the richness of the overlapping textures in the central portion of each drawing.

In view number four the strong directional quality is terminated with the view of the capitol building in the distance.

Drawings by: Davis Bité

238

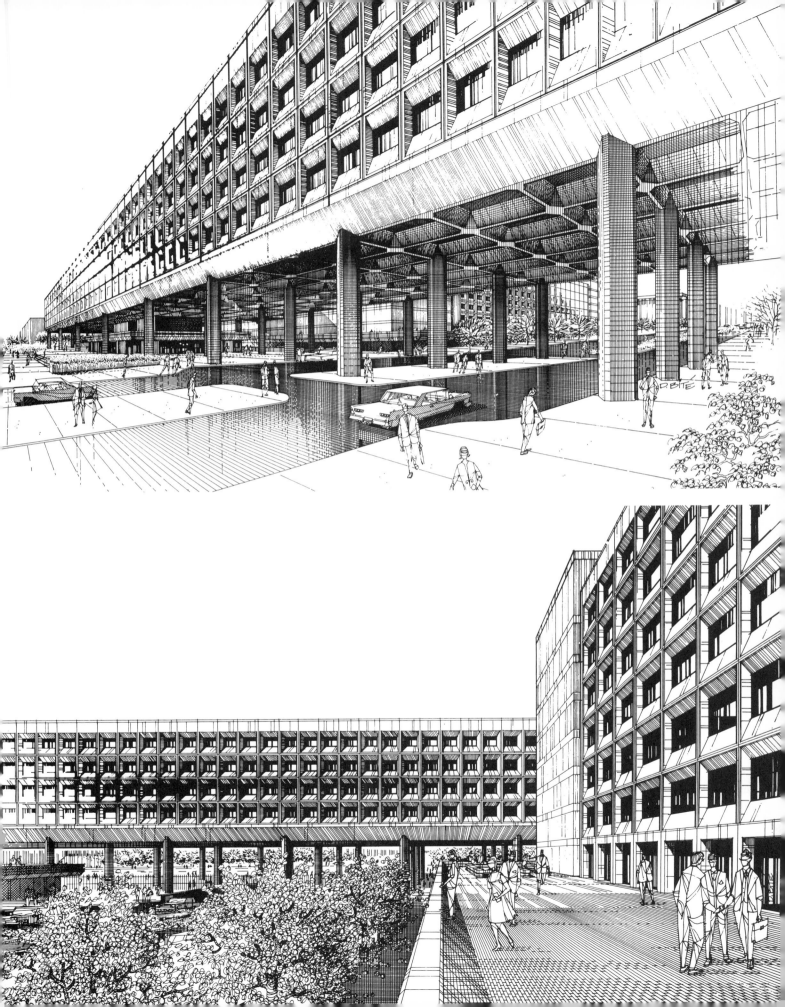

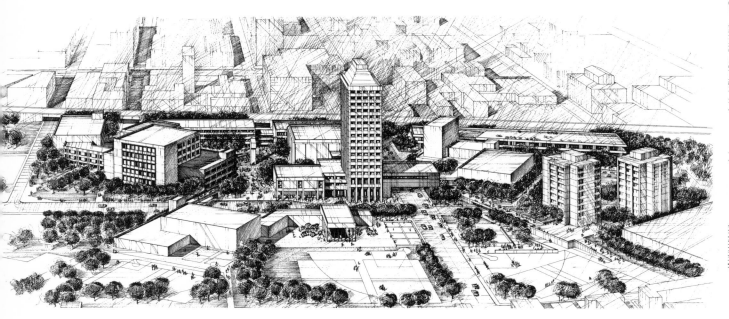

York University

Drawings by:
Mark deNalovy-Rozvadovski

This series demonstrates a campus in the conceptual stage without finalized architectural design. With this in mind certain moods were created by showing open spaces with buildings grouped around these spaces. This afforded enough of a view of the structures, yet allowed the creation of interest in the elements of entourage as well.

An interesting sequence is found in the two drawings showing the clock tower from nearly opposite positions. The activity of the students adds further interest and serves to link the series together. Further, the technique is kept consistently loose and open throughout.

60 State Street

Here the architecture becomes the unifying element. The strong shapes and design pattern of the precast units offer a striking element in each of the drawings. In addition, the new structure is set in a realistic setting clearly showing its relationship to the surrounding historic buildings. The aerial view and the overall ground-level view are taken from nearly the identical angle, thus establishing the site relationship clearly.

The technique used here was to render the project fully in pen and ink, then to treat the adjacent buildings lightly.

Drawings by:
Mark deNalovy-Rozvadovski

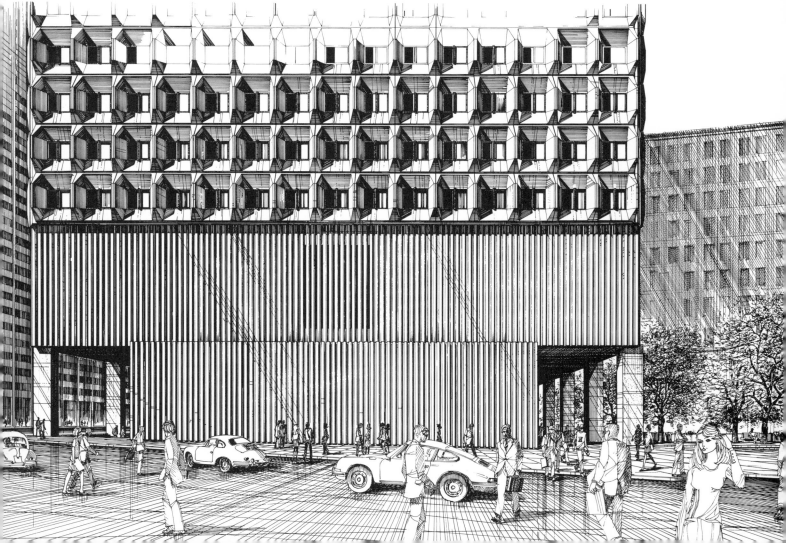

Pan Am Terminal

This series of pen and ink drawings was designed to illustrate several aspects of a major addition to an existing airport terminal building.

First several quick impression-istic sketches were executed di-rectly from photographs of the ex-isting terminal. These were intended to give the same impression as one would experience in vehicular move-ment around the structure.

Next a more detailed view of the new addition demonstrated the scale of part of the structure in relation to the commercial airplanes and the attending apron activity.

This was followed by an interior view of a typical gate lounge. A uni-fying element with the exterior view was created by showing the airplane in its gate position.

The exterior aerial view then showed all airplanes in their gate positions and related the new addi-tion not only to the existing terminal but to the entire surroundings.

Worcester Center

The unifying element in this series of watercolor renderings is the focus on the central group of buildings planned for a redeveloped downtown area. The viewpoints were carefully changed in each drawing to show different aspects of the grouping.

In the ground-level view emphasis was placed on the main structure and the entourage of the adjoining plaza. Then the angle was changed to view the complete project in relation to some nearby existing landmarks. Finally, the aerial view was shown from still another direction, and this time other existing structures as well as some proposed new structures were shown.

Drawings by: Ron Love

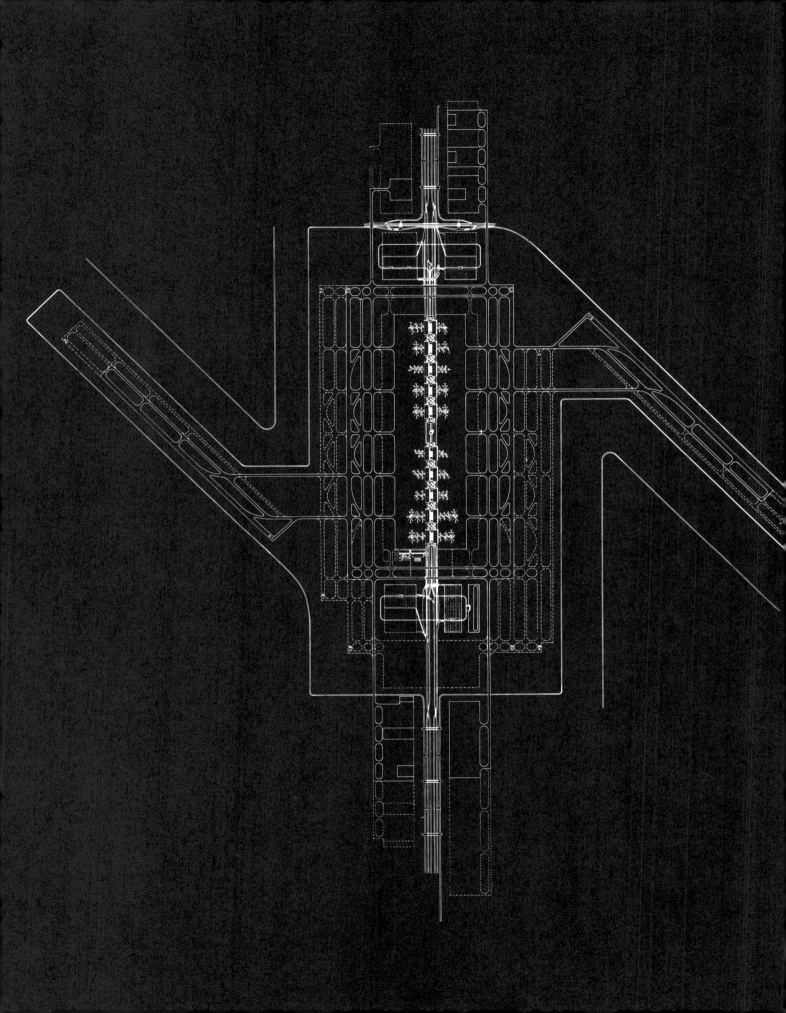

Dallas-Ft. Worth Airport

The only viewpoint that can represent structures that are the size of major airports is the aerial viewpoint. However, models are generally more descriptive from an aerial viewpoint than are renderings. The model, however, cannot be shown in section. The sectional perspective, then, can be a necessary device for showing portions of large spaces.

The overall design concept for this airport involved a series of structures that could be constructed along a linear spine which of course became the major element for access. In order to show portions of this linear spine, certain devices were necessary.

The major unifying element became the transit system which appears in each of the renderings.

Drawings by: Ron Love

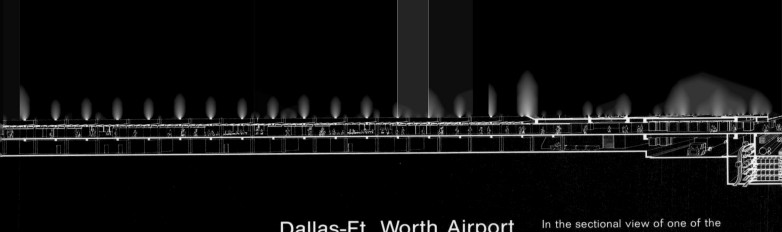

Dallas-Ft. Worth Airport

In the sectional view of one of the parking structures and air terminal wings the complex interrelationships of functions are clearly expressed. Baggage handling, utilities, and transportation are each expressed.

Drawings by: Ron Love

The sectional perspectives amplify different segments along the spine. By limiting the colored portion of the drawing to the center area, the attention is focused on the elements within the structure.

This series was executed over a period of time and was produced by two people using the same technique. Each was executed in pen and ink and the values put in with airbrush. This large complex involved three major buildings, each one connected by an enclosed pedestrian bridge. Each drawing emphasizes a different building, yet shows each of the other two.

The two aerial views were produced at different stages of design development. The first drawing shows the entire complex from a high vantage point with emphasis on the tower structure. The second, from a much lower vantage point, places the emphasis on the group relationship of three buildings, including the tower. The ground-level view of the tower (1) shows its relationship to the street and existing train station.

Gateway

PENN STATION

4. Drawing by: Brian Burr

5. Drawing by: Brian Burr

Gateway

A view from inside the pedestrian bridge provides a detailed view of a plaza and fountain, and the section perspective shows the bridge in its entirety. The final view is of the hotel with the tower in the background. In each drawing the existing train station and connecting pedestrian bridges provided the link.

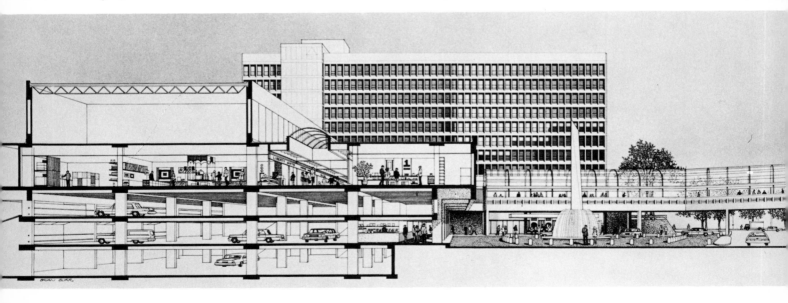

6. Drawing by: Ernest Burden

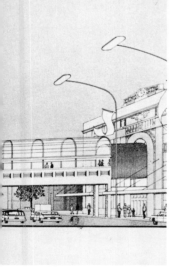

Lawrence Hall of Science

This series of drawings, executed in pen and ink, was produced for entry in an architectural competition. Plans, elevations, sections, and perspectives were all related by technique.

Included in the presentation were two exterior perspectives. The basis for both perspective drawings was an aerial photograph of the entire area. It was decided to render them in that same overall format rather than enlarge the actual project area to a more standardized size.

Thus, each drawing had to make use of certain compositional devices to emphasize the actual project. Main arterial roads provided the compositional element in the aerial. Certain dominant and recognizable features of the university campus were emphasized to provide a unifying element within the series of drawings.

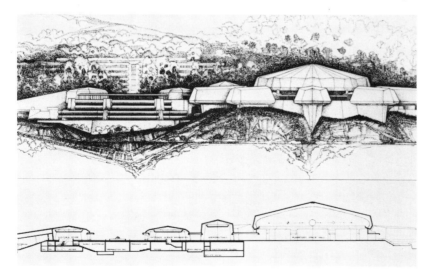

Lawrence Hall of Science

PART FOUR
Presentation

Chapter 11

Model photography

Realistic scale model photography requires a thorough knowledge of camera technique as well as the ability to recreate natural lighting effects.

Some models are built for presentation with no immediate plans for photographing. Though the model adapts to most photographic views, some shots may be impractical because of various obstructions. Surrounding buildings in the model may obstruct certain low views of the main building. The model frame itself may interfere with the camera or hinder low shots. Other models are built for presentation but intentionally designed with photography in mind. It is this type of model that will be discussed in this chapter.

Dalton Residence

Many considerations must be given to scale model photography, but foremost among them is that of lighting the model.

Proper lighting can either highlight or subdue a certain texture or form. Lighting can also be used to dramatize certain aspects of the design.

Backgrounds are extremely important in model photography. The most common one used by photographers is either black or white, depending on the mood desired.

A natural side effect of lighting, other than the rendition of textures, is the pattern of shadows produced by the direction of the lighting.

Photography in the studio allows better control of these various aspects. Shadows and the direction of light can be purposefully and very carefully studied.

On study models, such as the one shown here, lighting should be maneuvered in such a way that construction defects in the model do not become glaring distractions.

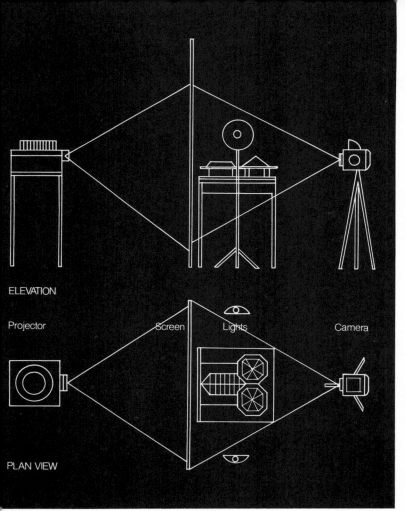

ELEVATION

Projector   Screen   Lights   Camera

PLAN VIEW

Edgewood Park

In photographing a model indoors, many lighting arrangements are possible, but the most realistic is that which simulates an outdoor sunny day. This means a primary source of light.

The background must receive more light than the model itself (except that some small highlights on the model may be the brightest part of the picture). Lighting should usually be brighter on the background than on the model because it creates the feeling of atmosphere and distance beyond the model.

One of the major advantages of indoor photography is the ability to put virtually any background behind the model. By using slides in an ordinary slide projector, any background can be projected realistically behind the model.

Placing actual photographs behind the model will probably prove too costly. To produce a photo of the size needed would take extra-large paper and the result would be too grainy to be effective. The most common method of projecting the background behind the model is to place a translucent screen between the slide projector and the model. In this way, the image can appear closely behind the model for better focusing. Commercially made rear projection screens are available, but they are expensive. A good-quality vellum paper will work well as a screen. Mounting the paper in a frame of illustration board will keep it in position. After setting up the model and the background, the model lighting should be arranged. Light meter readings of both the back projected screen light and the model light should be taken. This can be done by turning off all the room lights except the projected background slide, while taking the reading. Then the projector is shut off and a reading is taken of the model lighting. Exposures for each condition are calculated and recorded for later use. With the camera set up, all lights in the room are turned off and the camera shutter is opened. The projector is then turned on for the time calculated previously then turned off again. This records the background only on the film. The model, which has stayed dark, will not yet appear. The screen is then removed from behind the model since it would appear white with the lights shining on the model and wash out the background. Then the model lights are turned on again and an exposure made on the same frame of film (*note:* the film has not been advanced yet), with the model in the same position. Several different backgrounds could be used to see which one fits the scene best. Pictures of the actual site can be taken beforehand with this in mind.

It is wise either to regulate the model lights and the projector light with timers or to leave the projector light on and use the timed shutter in the camera. Experimentation will prove helpful, but be sure to make a record of your exposures.

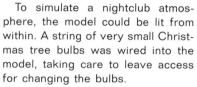

The Red Balloon

This model was built for a dual purpose, photography and presentation. Although it was built primarily for presentation, it was intentionally designed with the camera in mind. With this added convenience, the camera can be more versatile. The model was constructed so that the top was removable, thus allowing unlimited viewing of the entire room. Certain walls were also removable so the camera could shoot interior spaces.

To simulate a nightclub atmosphere, the model could be lit from within. A string of very small Christmas tree bulbs was wired into the model, taking care to leave access for changing the bulbs.

The model was built at a scale of ½ inch to the foot, which made the interior detail large enough to be clearly seen. The materials used in such a model should be carefully considered because some materials will not photograph well and tend to spoil the effect of realism.

The main interior elements were built of balsa wood and cardboard. Walls which were to receive murals in the final scheme were treated similarly in the model in miniature. Photostats of the mural designs were reduced down to the scale of the model. The scale figures used were modeled out of clay and painted to make them as realistic as possible.

The seating arrangement was easily constructed by covering metal washers with multicolored velvet disks, which represented groups of colorful cushioned seats. Carpet was simulated by using the same velvet. Metal scroll work on the gazebos was achieved by drawing the metal design on both sides of a sheet of acetate and then carefully cutting out the entire shape. Since the top and each of two sides were built to be removable, a number of views could be taken with the camera without disturbing or removing any part of the interior of the model.

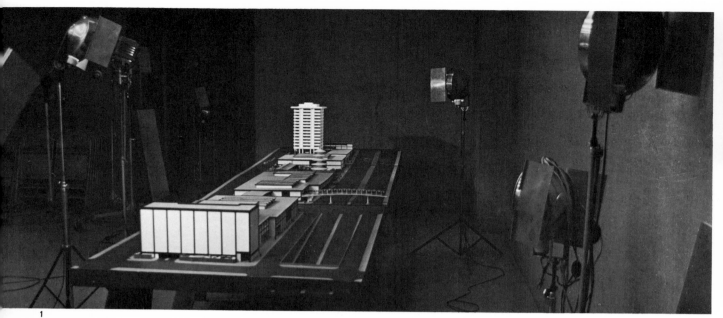

1

Japanese Center

2

3

4

The equipment needed for professional model photography is generally expensive. In a typical studio setup you will find tripods capable of holding a camera in practically any position, lights on movable booms, photoflood lamps with barn doors for deflecting the light, and focusing spotlights with a variable spread of light. This equipment is necessary to professional photographer (1).

One of the many assets of indoor photography is that the work is not subject to weather conditions. Models can always be photographed indoors. The lighting, which is so important, can be controlled indoors to acquire the right shadows, light and dark areas, and textures to suit the situation.

When photographing a model in a particular setup, take more than one picture of it. This is easily accomplished by using an elevator head tripod. Once you see the finished print, you may feel that a view slightly higher or one slightly lower might have been a more appropriate choice. Lighting for a sequence like this would be accomplished by keeping a strong light on the model, with the rest of the room lights off. This will make the background appear black in the photograph (2,3,4).

A characteristic of the conventional drawn elevation or roof plan

8

is its flatness or lace of perspective. These views are easier drawn flat than in perspective and shadows are used to define the near and far plane on the model. The camera ordinarily "sees" in perspective as the human eye does; therefore, it would put perspective in the elevation or roof plan. The camera can also make these shots "flat," as they would be drawn, by moving back (5) from the model or by using a Telephoto lens.

When photographing from a distance to eliminate the perspective, there are several considerations. First, because the model is farther away from the camera, it will not fill the frame. The print will have to be enlarged, meaning a possible loss in quality of the final photo. Focusing will have to be done carefully on this type of shot because the enlarging will magnify any out-of-focus condition.

Look for viewpoints that could possibly be coordinated with actual site conditions. This may mean a little extra planning, but the results will be worth the effort (8,9).

As is true with all specialized work, the photography of architectural models often depends on ingenuity and creativeness to produce the effects that make it such a valuable presentation tool.

6

7

9

1

Japanese Center

There are two basic types of model photography: natural and unnatural. Natural photography attempts to put the model in a natural setting. With the unnatural method certain contrived lighting effects are used. You can create many different lighting effects, such as the series shown here (1,2,3,4). The pagoda shape was the main focal element. By changing the background lighting, the row of flags was first rendered normal, then highlighted, and finally silhouetted.

2

3

There are other things that can be done with a picture of the model, using photography. By taking a dramatic picture of a model and printing the negative through a pre-arranged screen, you can obtain startling results.

The end result will be a photograph which resembles a very detailed, very meticulous, textured rendering.

Here photography has run the full course by attempting to make your photograph look like a drawing.

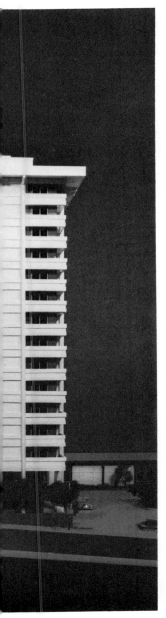

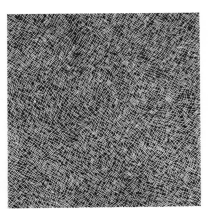

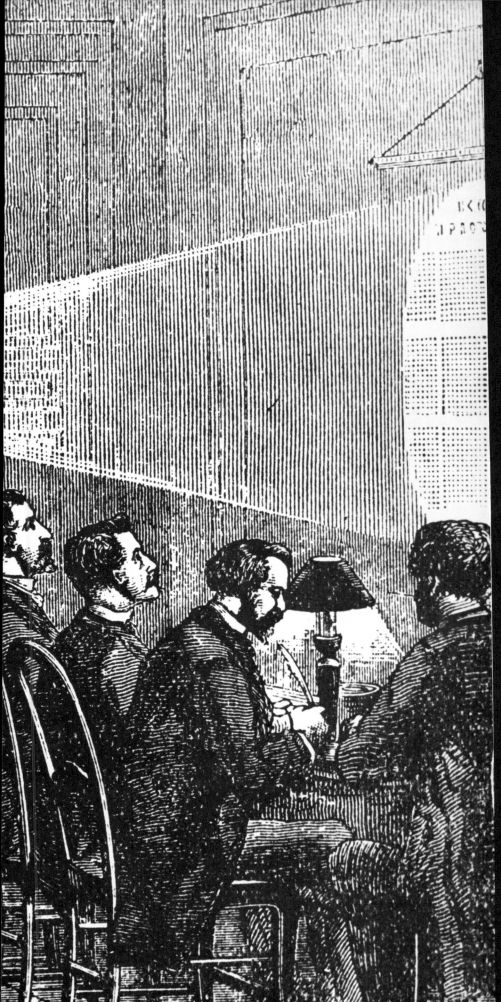

Chapter 12

Slide presentation

Often the complaint is raised that a slide presentation is too "jazzy" an approach to sell a design idea. The architect has prepared plans, elevations, and sections, and has hired a colored rendering done of his project. This, he feels, is all that is necessary or even desirable to present his project to a client. However, a true presentation has a much broader base and therefore a much broader area of appeal. In a presentation you can use the spoken word, the written word, statistics, pictures, renderings, plans, models, site photos, and anything else that you feel is appropriate. In short, a slide presentation can become a totally creative tool in the hands of an imaginative person.

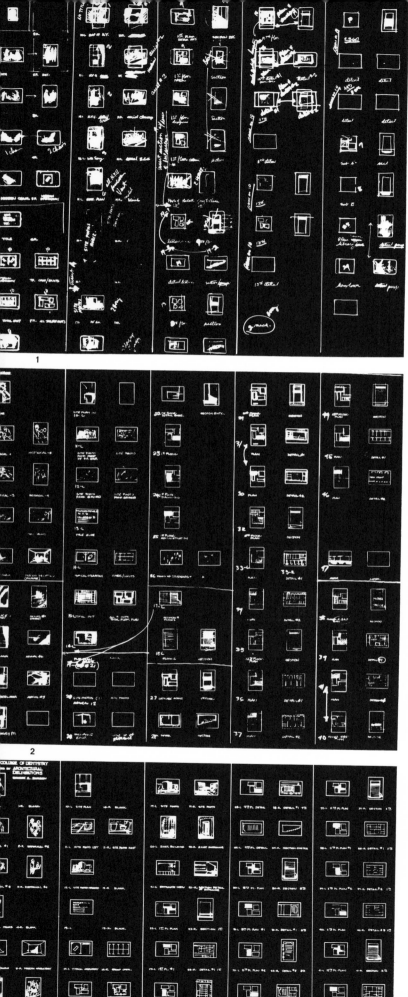

1

2

3

The Storyboard

The first step in any presentation is planning the show. Plan a show that will run about 12 minutes, no longer. This is the actual amount of program in a quarter-hour TV show. Try to tell your story with 80 slides, no more. This amount is about all you have time to show in 12 minutes.

You can begin to plan your show with a device used for many years by the movie and television industry, called the storyboard. This device makes it possible to plan an entire show in any amount of detail and for any number of slides.

First you will need a master sheet to guide you in programming your show. The best way to make one is to rule off a sheet of 2x2 frames and draw within these frames both the horizontal and vertical slide formats, plus a square format for superslides if you are going to use them (4).

With this as an underlay sheet, begin to plan your show. Start with the opening sequence; when this is settled, do the closing sequence; then fill in between. The most important parts of the show and the most difficult to plan are the opening and closing sequences.

Once you have completed a rough storyboard, you will see slides that can be changed around and some that should be eliminated (1,2).

The storyboard shown here was set up for a double-image projection shown side by side. Therefore the storyboard was layed out in pairs of slides and each frame could be planned in relationship to the other. This storyboard also facilitated the numbering of the slides for their respective left and right projectors and the writing and keying of the script (3).

Your script is the mortar that will hold your slides together. For an 80-slide show that will run 12 minutes you will need a script of approximately 1,500 words. Before you actually begin writing, project all the slides in the order you plan to show them. Look at them alone the first time through. Then ad-lib a commentary about the slides as you project them. This will get you involved with the material, and you will begin to see how long each slide should be left on the screen. At this stage, the overall pattern of your show will begin to emerge. All this should take place before you have written a word. Write your show in short segments, showing about 10 or 12 slides at a time. Figure 15 or 20 words per slide and you will automatically end up with a 12-page script. There will be times when you will not want, or need, a caption for a particular slide. In this case a recorded musical background is helpful to provide continuity. Once you have all the captions written, read the script aloud. It will sound choppy at first. Smooth out the writing by analyzing the slides as you read. Strive especially for clarity and continuity.

The storyboard should be set up and designed according to the type of projection you are going to use. This one was designed to program a series of 54 super-slides shown in a lap-dissolve sequence (5).

4

5

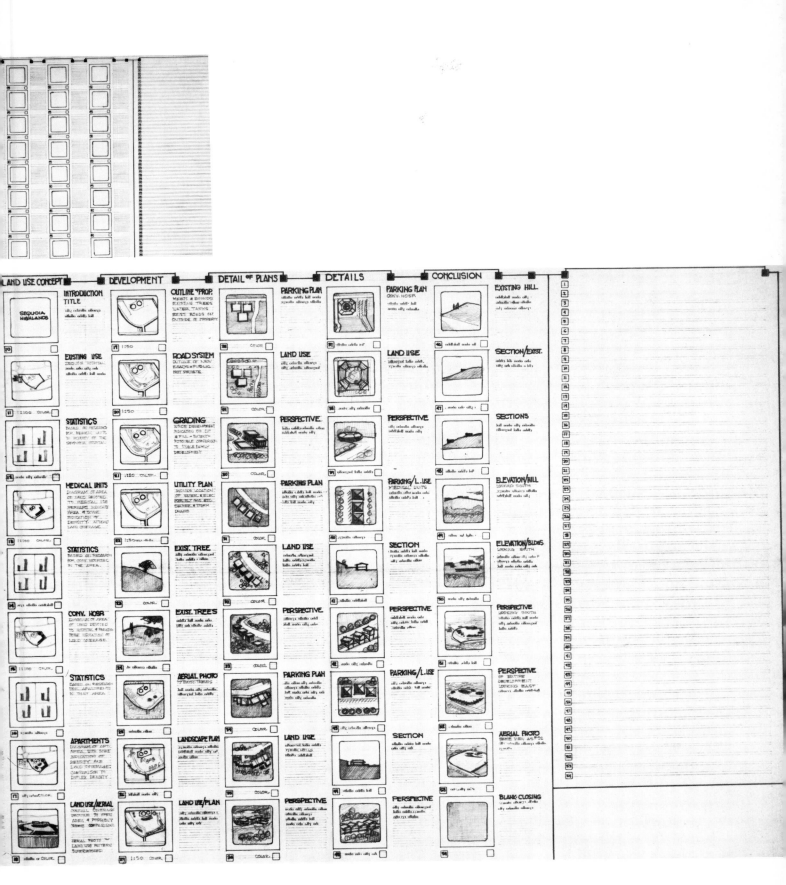

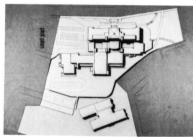

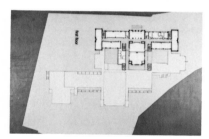

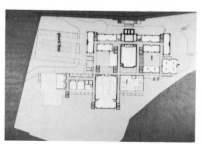

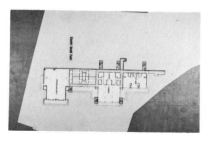

Mt. Vernon School

This show, presenting an addition to an existing school complex, was given for a small local school board. The addition would be carried out in successive stages. This gave rise to the idea of using a single projector capable of producing lap-dissolve images by using a special attachment on an ordinary projector. Before planning the sequence of slides, information was gathered as to what material was available for use. Architectural plans were all assembled and reduced to a small size for reviewing purposes. A trip to the site yielded many color slides of the existing school. Care was taken to be at the site during lunch recess in order to capture the school in active use.

After examining the material carefully, it was decided to investigate the availability of aerial photographs. This would allow the existing and future extensions to be shown from an aerial point of view. Instructions were sent to an aerial photographer for the desired views and possible altitudes. In addition to the usual black and white, the photographer took along a roll of color film for slides to be used in the presentation. With the materials in hand the storyboard was planned.

Using a study model of the pro-

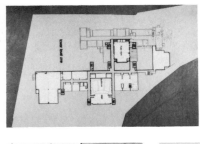

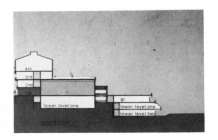

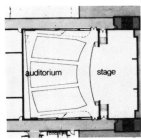

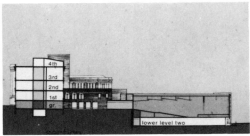

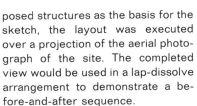

posed structures as the basis for the sketch, the layout was executed over a projection of the aerial photograph of the site. The completed view would be used in a lap-dissolve arrangement to demonstrate a before-and-after sequence.

Prior to this, however, it seemed desirable to show a series on stages of the development of the site plan. These plans were reduced to a workable size of 11 by 14 inches and colored with overlays. Following this sequence of floor plans was a series of elevations and related sectional views. Several details of the plans were put in for emphasis, and these were combined with quick sketches of certain interior spaces. These progressed through several stages, terminating with a comparison of the existing schoolyard and the new structure. To further emphasize this comparison, the existing schoolyard was shown in black and white and the sketches of the new addition, taken from the exact same angle, were projected in color.

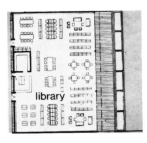

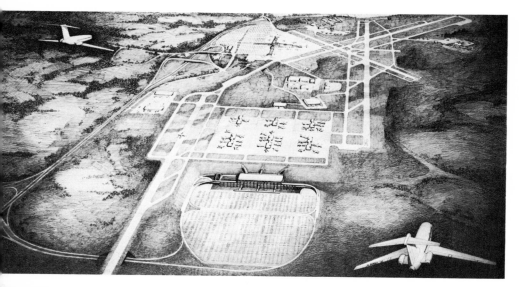

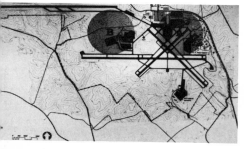

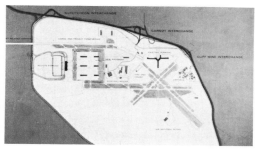

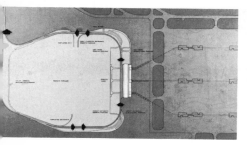

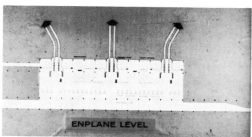

ENPLANE LEVEL

Greater Pittsburgh Airport

This slide presentation was designed to show a preliminary scheme for a major airport. The materials at hand were three colored renderings executed previously and many architectural plans.

Even good photographers have to learn a few new tricks before they can make good slides. The magnification of the image during projection shows up every defect, so slides have to be of better quality than pictures for direct viewing. Images must be exceedingly sharply focused. Exposures have to be just right, so it is a good practice to make a test exposure roll prior to actual shooting of the finished material. Dust and fingerprints glare out on the projection screen and distract the viewer.

There were so many considerations involving the planning and phasing of development that a dual-projection show was decided upon. This would reduce the time for showing, since two slides would be projected simultaneously, and would give the added advantage of allowing certain comparisons to be made. These comparisons could be various stages of site development, overall and detailed views of the terminal building or plan, and sectional views shown side by side. Additional sketches, which already existed from an earlier presentation, were used to provide stopping points.

Each of the drawings was photographed not only in its entire format but in detail as well, thus obtaining several slides from one rendering.

The storyboard produced for this show was used to further advantage in regard to the script for the show. The entire storyboard was broken down into segments that would fit on one side of an 8½- by 11-inch page, leaving the other side free for writing the commentary. Each pair of slides, left and right, were thus keyed very closely with the script. This enabled the show to be presented not only by the person who designed it but by others as well.

280

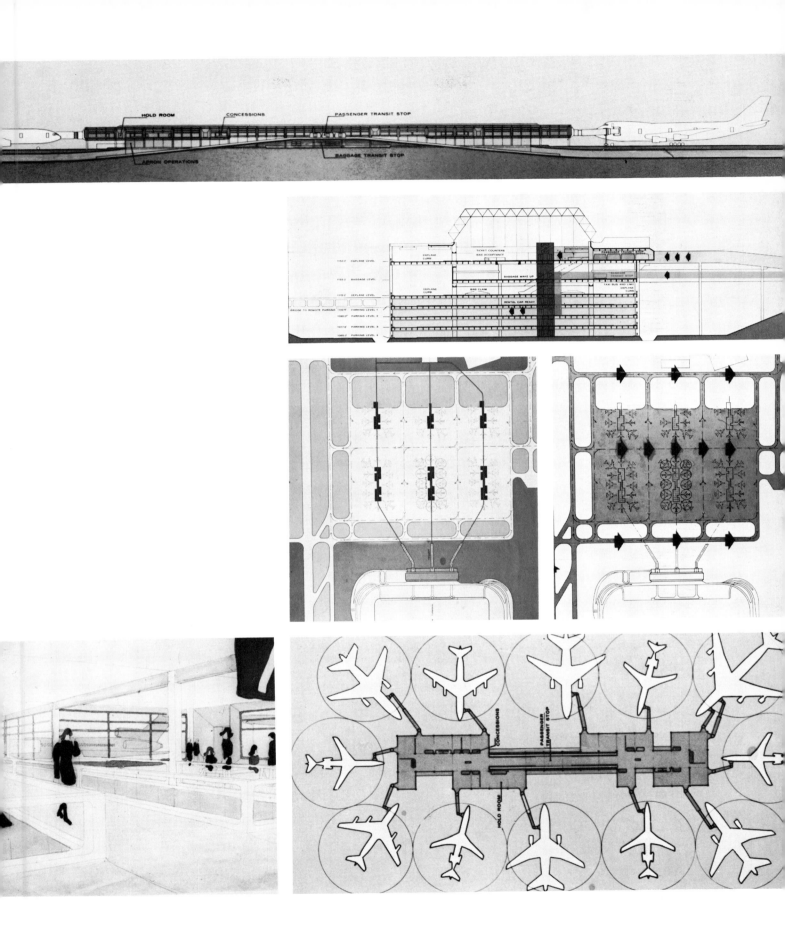

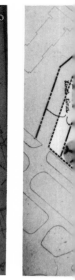

Pan Am Terminal

The first step in building a good slide show is to know exactly what you have to work with and what slides are available for use. This means careful picture taking, sorting, organizing, and filing for later use. One important note: Do not throw away any slide unless it is technically unusable. The slide you may be tempted to reject for photographic reasons may bring a positive response for quite a different reason when you weave it into your show.

When you visit a site for exploratory reasons, take a picture of everything that might be of even remote interest. Sometimes these can turn into key pictures. In the example shown here, it was decided that several night pictures might prove interesting. They were so effective that this sequence was used as the opening of the show. The next unplanned sequence resulted from an excursion into the construction area of the new addition to the terminal. Here the photo sequence of the workman, followed by the crane lifting steel plates into

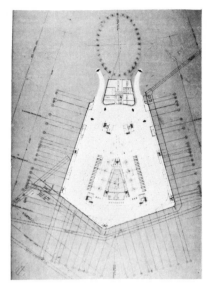
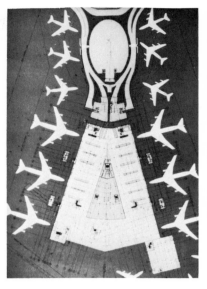

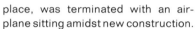

place, was terminated with an airplane sitting amidst new construction.

To complement these construction pictures, architectural plans were meticulously colored on reduced prints and photographed in sequence.

An architectural presentation model had been constructed much earlier and was put to additional use for this show. This particular model had been built in removable sections, thus enabling complete inspection of the multilevel structure, one floor at a time. A subminiature camera was actually placed inside the model for some environmental shots.

Lighting for the model was provided by a single-source quartz lamp with a focusing beam. The model was placed in a normally lit room, yet the use of this high-intensity light produced dark areas outside the model area. This is important because most slides of a model will contain some of the base or background of the model, which can be eliminated only by masking out.

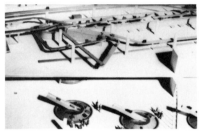

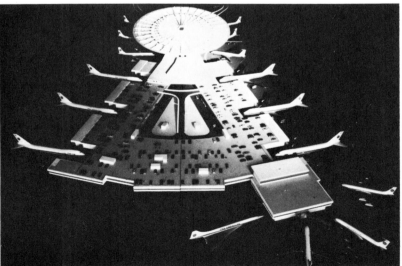

Wildflower

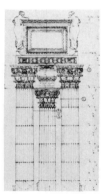

This show was designed for entry in a competition which stipulated that it had to be capable of being shown automatically at any time and place and with standard equipment. Therefore, an automatically timed projector was used and a tape recorder simultaneously carried the narration and musical background. The subject matter was the preservation of a historic landmark, photographically; and the ultimate reconstruction of this temporary building into a permanent form became part of the story.

The story began in 1915 when the Palace of Fine Arts was constructed for the Panama Pacific International Exposition. After the exposition closed, the entire fairgrounds were leveled except for the Palace of Fine Arts. The slide show then traced the history of the building from the very earliest days of construction, to the ultimate beauty of its full usefulness, then to its gradual fall into disuse.

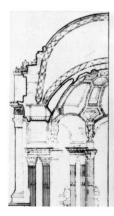

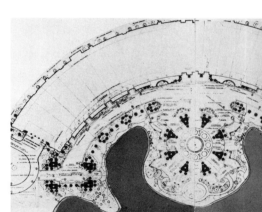
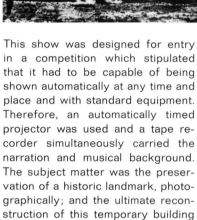

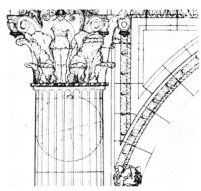

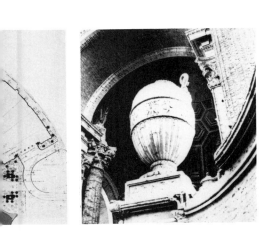

Wildflower

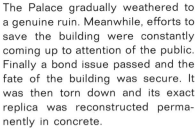

The Palace gradually weathered to a genuine ruin. Meanwhile, efforts to save the building were constantly coming up to attention of the public. Finally a bond issue passed and the fate of the building was secure. It was then torn down and its exact replica was reconstructed permanently in concrete.

At a cost of ten times the original and with no definite practical use established, it was an unprecedented civic investment in pure aesthetics which may never again be matched.

Thus two buildings had been preserved: one was preserved photographically and the reconstructed version preserved in permanent materials.

Façade

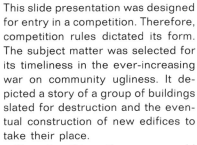

This slide presentation was designed for entry in a competition. Therefore, competition rules dictated its form. The subject matter was selected for its timeliness in the ever-increasing war on community ugliness. It depicted a story of a group of buildings slated for destruction and the eventual construction of new edifices to take their place.

To portray this on the screen would have required multiple projection, but the competition rules did not allow this; nor could the show run for more than a specified short period of time. Therefore, all the photographs selected for the show were prearranged, cut out, and mounted on

black cardboard. Then the composite was photographed on one single 35mm frame. This allowed up to 250 pictures to be shown on 80 single 35mm slides. Certain parts of the slides were carefully masked to crop off any area not wanted on the composite slide. The end result was a multiple-image presentation using a single projector and a single slide each time. The possibilities of combinations using this approach are endless and the benefit, aside from the competition requirements, is an effective presentation tool without the cumbersome disadvantages of the arrangements necessary for multiple-projection presentations.

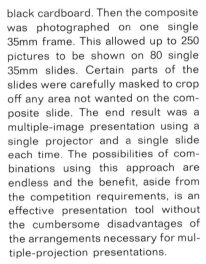

Chapter 13

Presentation to public agencies

Behind every good presentation is usually much experimentation, observation, selection, analysis, imagination, and work. When these presentations are brought before the public, whether it be a school board or a city planning commission, the show had better be polished to meet the occasion. It is often little items that can upset a program, embarrass the speaker, and distract the audience.

Advanced planning and rehearsals are as good insurance as anything against such disasters. The equipment should be in good working order, and the operation of all systems should be second nature. Familiarity with the subject is essential.

EDGEWOOD PARK

Edgewood Park

In planning a slide show to present before a council and audience, be sure you are familiar with the physical arrangement of the room and the graphic aids you will need. It is a good idea to rehearse your show in the same room either the night before or at least an hour before presenting it. The room you use will determine many aspects of the presentation. You should test all the equipment to see that it operates properly and have spare bulbs on hand for all projectors.

This particular presentation was designed to display the concept of a cluster development. It was very important to hold the attention of the audience and the planning commission members until the entire message had been presented. Therefore, the entire script was tape recorded and a musical background added to discourage interruptions, whether intentional or not, on the part of the audience. The lights were turned off,

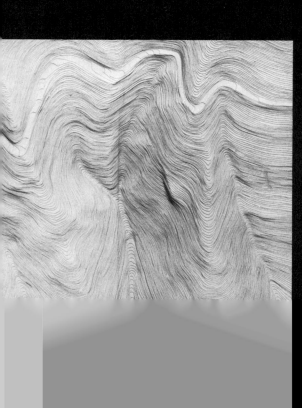

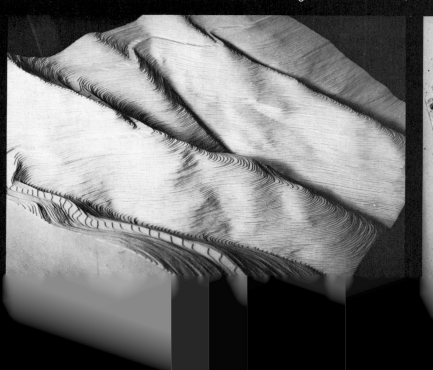

the recorder turned on, and the show was presented.

The use of a lap-dissolve projector provided visual continuity from one slide to the next. The screen is never black or white using this type of projector, which can be a distraction and produce eye strain. Here model and plans were effectively combined with actual site photos, thereby increasing the effect of realism of the proposed development. Site photos were dissolved into renderings done from the same vantage point.

The end result was a totally controlled presentation whereby the audience could easily understand the evolving design process. Had the designer simply shown up at the meeting with a colored rendering of the entire development and his plans and elevations, he would have had much more explaining to do than that which was very succinctly put forth in a 15-minute color slide presentation.

Sequoia Highlands

To present a proposal for a piece of property that had a history of stormy planning commission disapprovals is difficult enough. But to follow a citizens' committee armed with a 16mm color movie urging that the area not be developed at all could be disheartening. Such was the history of Motorcycle Hill, as it was commonly known for years.

The approach taken in presenting a new design concept for this hill was to illustrate as clearly and quickly as possible a logical solution for use of the land. In designing the presentation, therefore, it was of foremost importance to keep the orientation simple and direct. All plans, diagrams, perspectives, and photo-

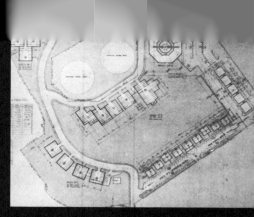

graphs were developed with the orientation reversed from the normal north at the top of the page to south at the top of the page. The reason for this reversal was that all those who had opposed the development faced the hill to the south of them. This orientation would then directly respect their concern.

The presentation was designed to be shown with lap-dissolve projection, which would provide a very smooth visual continuity for the sequential series.

First the main planning concepts were proposed by showing a series of graphics superimposed over an aerial vertical photograph of the site. Next came a series illustrating the development of the land-use concept, which began with a grading plan and the few existing trees. This was followed by a landscaping plan to illustrate future planned growth. This was followed by a rendered land-use plan, incorporating the new landscaping. From this beginning another series was shown beginning with a parking diagram to accommodate the number of dwelling units. This was followed by a rough model of the hill, yet still shown in plan view. The rough model dissolved to the total scheme in color, still shown in plan view. This would have been a logical place to end the slide presentation, but many questions remained unanswered.

Sequoia Highlands

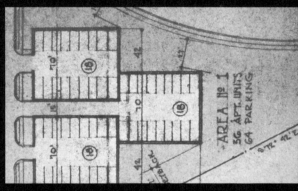

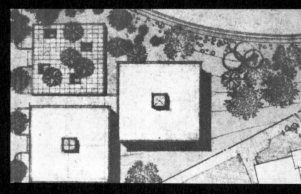

The model was again shown, but this time from the same viewpoint as the perspectives. The narration began by discussing details of the project by areas. Beginning with area 1, a series of slides was shown where the camera had taken detailed views of each drawing previously presented. The parking diagram was followed by the rendered land-use plan, this in turn was followed by the model, again in plan view. Next appeared a cross-sectional view of the area under discussion in the recorded narration. Following this came an aerial color slide of that particular area under discussion and a view of

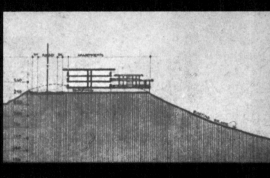

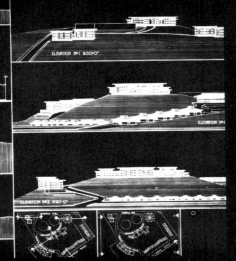

the model from the same relative vantage point. This same procedure was repeated twice more to cover the other areas in the same detailed manner. Finally, after every pertinent point was made concerning the concept, the development, and the implementation, the show was over. The whole presentation was made in less than 15 minutes yet explained a design concept that could have taken hours if a conventional approach had been taken.

Chapter 14

Reproduction and office promotion

Many aspects of office promotion involve the use or application of photography. Both the written word and the picture must be transferred by some photomechanical means to the printed page. Therefore, reproduction problems and techniques are primary considerations in planning for promotional material to be published.

Photography must be used to record the progress and completion of the construction of a building.

When this material is compiled and organized properly, it can be put to additional use as promotional material. Every presentation tool created to explain your project to a client can also be used to promote your own services.

Office Promotion—Reproduction

If an accurate record is kept of every site, rendering, model, and every other aspect of the construction of a project, it is an easy matter to further amplify your public relations program with slide or film presentations. There are countless occasions when these presentations might be appropriate to show to a civic group, a local planning board, or a potential client.

One of the most appropriate places to have a presentation of your own work is in your own office. This type of slide show need not run continuously, yet it could be arranged in such a way that a simple push of a button started it to run. Many fully automatic and variable self-timed projectors are available for this kind of use. The most successful system would incorporate back projection, so the equipment would not be visible. Easy access must be provided to change or repair any part of the setup.

Each project can easily be arranged in its own slide tray, properly marked, and stored for easy retrieval. In addition to this a properly indexed slide file is necessary for those slides not used in the presentation tray. On any important project those slides used in the presentation should be duplicated first to avoid loss or misplacement. Slides from one presentation should not be borrowed from another previously set up tray, since it is easy to forget to replace them. Then when a presentation is given, it will be incomplete.

The proper architectural presentation should receive the same care and attention as the design of any of your projects. It should be designed with certain definite promotional ideas or explanations in mind. This is somewhat different from the slide shows described earlier, as those specialized on one particular project. The slide show for promotional use must be well thought out, carefully programmed, and professionally executed. The message concerns your image and your capabilities and nothing less than the best should be considered.

As most people realize, it is usually more difficult to create something for yourself than for your clients. If this is the case, it would be worthwhile hiring someone who specializes in the area of public relations to set the guidelines for material to be contained in the presentation. This material should then be interpreted and executed by someone who creates slide or film presentations professionally.

The reproduction camera in its modern form is one of the most spectacular pieces of photographic apparatus, so it is interesting to remember that it is just an elaboration of the camera obscura, described in the first chapter of this book. This type of camera has long been used for copy work and provides the highest quality reproduction available.

Anyone who has made a photographic copy of a drawing knows that there is some loss of detail, tonal gradation, and overall quality. Any published reproduction of this drawing is at best a reasonable facsimile of the original work. The degree of resemblance to the original will depend on the method of reproduction, the skill of the printer, and the quality of the original.

There are really only two major methods of reproduction: line and tone. Halftone is just a means of reducing tones to a dot pattern. Within this framework, halftone screens are available in variations from coarse to ultrafine. In addition to this there are many screens for special effects such as etchtones and mezzotints.

Except for several specialized methods of reproduction such as collotype or silk screen, which are limited to fairly short runs, most reproductions in quantity are accomplished by one of three major methods: letterpress; lithography; and offset, which is the most commonly used.

DESIGN CREDITS

Index